My Sacred Bull - 1

Insights into

Science and Spirituality

In Arrangement with *Financial Chronicle*

My Sacred Bull - 1

Insights into Science and Spirituality

In Arrangement with *Financial Chronicle*

Kuruvilla Pandikattu SJ
Professor of Physics, Philosophy and Religion
Jnana-Deepa Vidyapeeth, Pune

CWI
Christian World Imprints(TM)

First Published in 2015 by

Christian World Imprints(TM)
Christian Publishing & Books from India
H-12 Bali Nagar, **New Delhi-110015**
info@christianworldimprints.com
www.ChristianWorldImprints.com
Phone: +91 11 25465925 Fax: +91 11 25173055

ISBN-13: 978-93-5148-008-2 ISBN-10: 93-5148-008-9

Cataloging in Publication Data--DK
Courtesy: D.K. Agencies (P) Ltd. <docinfo@dkagencies.com>

Pandikattu, Kuruvilla.
Insights into science and spirituality in arrangement with Financial Chronicle / Kuruvilla Pandikattu.
p. cm.
Includes bibliographical references (p.) and index.
ISBN 9789351480082
ISBN 9351480089

1. Spiritual life. 2. Religion and science. 3. Religion and sociology. I. Title.

DDC 204.4 23

Printed at Chawla Offset Printers

Dedicated to:

My Colleague and Mentor,
Rev. Jose Elampassery SJ

The Book

Open-minded and visionary, these articles are meant to touch the daily life of busy people who are fully involved in the struggle and success of their life. These spiritual essays attempt to provide the readers with both roots and wings: roots that will give them a sense of belonging to the rich Indian heritage and wings that will take them forward based on the spiritual depth.

The Author has segregated this spiritual quest into nine sections dealing with:

- Prayer and Spirituality
- God and Religion
- Humans and Body
- Reality and Paradox
- Difference and Devotion
- Wealth and Wisdom
- Self and Security
- Change and Violence
- Science and Religion

These inspiring articles enshrine spiritual depth and religious openness, reflecting on science and spirituality; are not only for business leaders, managers, corporate executives, anthropologists, philosophers, theologists, researchers, institutions and libraries; but also for general audience, who may or may not be organisationally religious. They are meant to inspire a band of young men and women to think deeply about themselves, leading to deeper insights and wisdom.

These spiritually focused articles of the Author, appeared in the "My Mind" Editorial Page of the *Financial Chronicle* (www.mydigitalfc.com)

The Author

Dr. Kuruvilla Pandikattu (born 1957-) is Professor of Physics, Philosophy and Religion at Jnana-DeepaVidyapeeth, Pune, India, since 1996. He has three Masters' Degrees in Physics and Philosophy and two Doctorates in Philosophy and Theology to his credit. He has been actively involved in dialogue between science and religion. Author of more than 30 books and 160 academic articles, Pandikattu is a Jesuit priest belonging to Dumka-Raiganj Province, India. He has been involved in organising more than 20 national and international conferences on Science-Religion Dialogue. He has visited more than 15 countries and attended more than 100 conferences on Philosophy, Theology and Science-Religion Dialogue. Because of his creative and committed writings, he has been in the editorial board of five philosophical/religious journals. He is a renowned author, spiritual leader, motivational speaker and research guide. His main topics of research are: Anthropology, Eschatology and Transhumanism. He may be contacted at kuru@kuru.in (personal) or kuru@jdv.edu.in (professional). Site: www.kuru.in

Foreword

Six years ago, *Financial Chronicle*, India's first global business networking platform, was looking for spiritually focused, knowledge-driven content to inspire and enrich its educated audience of business leaders, managers and corporate executives. Editor-in-chief Shubhrangshu Roy, who conceived the daily newspaper and initiated the project "My Sacred Bull," on the editorial page of Financial Chronicle, asked me to discover an enlightened thinker to address the existential yearnings of intelligent India and FC's wider global audience.

I turned to Professor Kuruvilla Pandikattu SJ for his innate wisdom. He is a priest, physicist and philosopher, adorned with three masters' degrees and two doctorates. His creative spirit and open vision had long inspired me. The professor-priest readily obliged, taking pen to paper week after week to script a volume that has now acquired epic proportions. His pathbreaking column is deeply relished and respected by FC's global band of dedicated readers.

Prof Pandikattu's articles stand out for three characteristics that uncommon in both spiritual and scientific discourses:

Contextual sensitivity: Normally he takes up a current event – from politics, science or religion – and reflects on it giving it a spiritual basis and contemporary relevance.

Religious openness: Committed to his Catholic faith, his critical and creative acceptance of other religious and non-religious traditions is extraordinary. Without falling into eclecticism, he has a way of drawing the positive aspect of every event.

Forward movement: His writings pursue our quest as individuals and communities, to move ahead in our pilgrimage of life, conquering new peaks. He is convinced that the Spirit is working within us to move us to another level, where human beings can live in peace and harmony, affirming and respecting the differences that exist among each other.

By and large, these spiritual essays are non-denominational and are not limited to any religious group. At the same time, they open the inquisitive spirit in us and thus widen our experience. As such, his columns are very inspiring and forward-looking.

I am happy to note that he has handpicked the best of the first hundred articles that he has scripted for FC and is publishing them in this book: "My Sacred Bull : Insights into Science and Spirituality in arrangement with *Financial Chronicle*." As of today more than 200 well-appreciated articles of Prof Pandikattu have appeared in our "My Sacred Bull" column, which has been appearing in the "My Mind" section of *Financial Chronicle* for six years now. Truly a great achievement! I recommend this book whole-heartedly for its inquisitiveness, spiritual depth and universal openness.

Dr. Michael Gonsalves
Senior Assistant Editor
Financial Chronicle

Acknowledgements

In bringing out this book, I am immensely grateful to Mr. Shubhrangshu Roy, the Chief Operating Editor and Editor-in-chief of *Financial Chronicle (FC)*, who approached me to write these articles.

I am also indebted to Dr. Michael Gonsalves, Senior Assistant Editor of *Financial Chronicle*, who has been constantly urging me to contribute my share to it.

With a deep sense of gratitude, I want to acknowledge the role played by the staff and students of Papal Seminary, Pune and Jnana-Deepa Vidyapeeth, Pune, India, for providing me with the facilities and opportunities for these insights.

Finally, I am indeed grateful to the Almighty, who makes all things happen, so that we may "live, move and have our being" in Him, who is our Everything.

Kuruvilla Pandikattu SJ

Contents

Humans and Body

Reality and Paradox

Difference and Devotion

Wealth and Wisdom

Self and Security

Change and Violence

Science and Religion

Introduction

It is said that sex and spirituality are the most sought after themes in the internet. Human longing for self-realisation and meaning is part of people's spiritual quest. This book focuses on relevant spiritual insights for contemporary women and men.

The articles in this book are especially written for *Financial Chronicle* (FC), from the Hyderabad-based Deccan Chronicle Holdings Ltd, which was launched on 16 April, 2008, by India's youngest team of media professionals, and in the shortest-ever run-up for a newspaper.

As such each article is meant for a general audience, who may or may not be organisationally religious. They are meant to inspire a band of young men and women to think deeply about themselves, leading to deeper insights and wisdom.

Open-minded and visionary, these articles are meant to touch the daily life of busy people who are fully involved in the struggle and success of daily life. So the articles are limited to 625 words. And these articles attempt to provide them with both roots and wings: roots that will give them a sense of belonging to the rich Indian heritage and wings that will take them forward based on the spiritual depth.

Though the author gladly acknowledges his Christian commitment, he does not presuppose it from the audience. The Indian context of the author may be also evident from some of the examples or illustrations in the articles. Trying to be objective and philosophical, as much as possible, the articles are an open invitation to search for deeper meaning and widen vision.

For better clarity and convenience, these articles are divided into nine approximate and arbitrary sections.

I. Prayer and Spirituality
II. God and Religion
III. Humans and Body
IV. Reality and Paradox
V. Difference and Devotion
VI. Wealth and Wisdom
VII. Self and Security
VIII. Change and Violence
IX. Science and Religion

The presupposition of these articles is that spiritual life has to be based on day to day experiences of ordinary people and so God has to be found in our daily life. When we reflect on daily events, we have to truly be open to the deepest mystery that guides us forwards. A cautious and courageous attitude is necessary in this search. Truly optimistic and open-ended, these articles urge the readers to find the depth of existence in the ordinary things of the world and thus make the sacred emerge from the mundane. In that sense, even though some of us refuse to believe in God, as a species, we can claim to have a sacred space: in fact the only place where we can be on our own. Can we extend that space to the whole universe, including the heart of our neighbour? That, I believe is the crucial spiritual question of the day.

Prayer and Spirituality

1

A Five-step Prayer for Busy People

In today's hectic world, there is one short prayer that is quite relevant. A Spanish mystic, Ignatius Loyola, introduced this prayer. He recommended to his companions a daily method of examining their lives so that they might better serve the Lord with joy. He taught them the two keys to healthy spirituality: Find God in all things and constantly work to gain internal freedom to reach out to people.

St Ignatius proposed a daily exercise called examination of conscience or better consciousness. Examination of conscience gives the impression of looking within and finding one's faults and shortcomings. But examination of consciousness implies that one grows in spiritual sensitivity and is helped to recognise and receive God's presence in the world. Ignatius urged his brethren not to eliminate this one prayer and engage in it every single day. It is a simple prayer for busy people.

The five steps involved in this 15-minute prayer are: Recall oneself in the presence of God. Look at one's day with gratitude. Ask for help from the ever-present Divine source. Review the day. Reconcile and resolve to be more loving and compassionate.

The fourth point is crucial. Here, one carefully examines one's actions, omissions, thoughts and desires that tell one about his or her relationship with God and with the self and others. Each one of us can find a good way to do this. Sometimes, a single event stands out dramatically; for instance, one can lose temper or feel great joy at a piece of news. Patiently, one should ask oneself what one's action or attitude meant. Did it embody love of God, or fear or distrust?

At other times, no event stands out, but we might find a pattern emerging in the day; for instance, all day long one can feel anxious and worried; every time one sees a certain person, one may want to draw his or her attention. Patiently, ask yourself what that pattern means about your belief in God. At other times, the climate of life might emerge as clear as the day's weather; for instance, one may have grown dissatisfied with one's work; or find oneself shaking off an old resentment. This way, one deepens one's awareness of God's loving gaze on oneself. Patiently, one must ask what this shows about oneself and God.

This small prayer is at the heart of the spirituality developed by the Jesuits. If practised once or twice daily, it will help us to move closer to the divine will and sensitise us to His presence in everything. The point is to find the sources that tie us down in life — old habits, people, situations, conditions — that lead us to make cramped choices against life and love.

The more we notice how we can change and move towards God like flowers to the sun, the freer we become. And God continuously labours within us to make us more like Him. In this way, we can truly discern God in everything — including the person one hates, the evil one suffers and in the ordinary things of life. Thus, it is the examination of consciousness that helps us to foster a healthy spirituality, whereby one can discern God's presence even in the most mundane things.

2

Sex, the Soul and Spiritual Limits

Research shows that in the internet two of the most popular topics are sex and spirituality. Though they seem to be contradictory, they represent two fundamental human realities. Right from the beginning of human history, there have been strong tendencies to relate both and also to disengage one from the other. In Indian tradition, tantrism stands for a strong bond between sex and spirituality. While the advaitic tradition stands for a strict separation between the two.

Recently Donna Freitas (Freitas 2008) authored a book, *Sex and the Soul: Juggling Sexuality, Spirituality, Romance, and Religion on America's College Campuses.* Her book traced the dissonance between what the students wanted for themselves — meaningful relationships, romance (which they construe as asexual) — and what they felt everyone else wanted: partying and hooking up. It's all part of the dynamics that drive what Freitas calls the "hook-up culture" that can be traced to the American college campuses. That permissiveness has left many students looking for something that might just bring parents back from the edge.

"There's the peer campus culture, where students assume that what everybody wants is this sexually permissive culture," Freitas says. "But the vast majority of the students who promote and buy into this culture don't like it for themselves. They think people don't take sex seriously enough. They're not comfortable with the behaviour they see on campus" (Freitas 2008).

That dissatisfaction, she thinks, is at the root of a trend cited in recent studies: A resurgent interest in religion and spirituality among college students. She affirms further: "I found that lots of students were resisting traditional religion in many ways. They felt the teachings didn't make sense in their lives. They were latching on to spirituality as a space where they could hang on to meaning or search for it."

Their search for meaning took different forms, Freitas says, but it often revolved around struggles with sexual identity, with gender roles, and with what they were doing, and seeing others do, sexually. When she explored the dynamics between religion and sex on other college campuses, a remarkably consistent picture emerged. "Sex and the Soul" is made up of interviews with students. The book reveals that with the exception of evangelicals, students everywhere are encountering campus cultures that they feel far too sexually explicit, but they fear the consequences of standing against that culture and lack the guidance that might come from an open dialogue. Some students look to spirituality to help them navigate these waters, but privately; spiritual beliefs are rarely discussed in public.

> God continuously labours within us to make us more like Him.

She tells that "part of what I do is to provide students with possible structures around which to build a spiritual identity, some of which involve staking claims and drawing boundaries," she says: "I see in students an attraction to boundaries, even though that's what kicked them out of traditional religion in the first place."

Though the Indian situation is different, we can get significant insights from this book. Sex really needs a soul. The soul dimension or spirituality provides structures where we can enjoy sex within its own appropriate limits; where we can relish the physical within reasonable boundaries; where we can love both gently and firmly; where we can enjoy relationships in sustained and continued commitments.

3

An Era of Broader Spiritual Practice

Malta is a small island in the Mediterranean ocean. With a population of about four lakhs,[1] of whom 98 per cent are Christians, it is an ideal place to test the effect of economic growth and social progress on religion. Malta's entry into the European Union in 2004 and the scope for higher education have affected its religious orientation considerably.

University students have, on an average, 20 per cent less faith in the major Catholic beliefs than they did in 2003, according to a recent survey by the University Chaplaincy, of the same country. However, two out of every three respondents still accept the basic tenets of the Catholic faith. Still it is seen the students' faith in the church dropped dramatically, from 75 per cent in 2003 to 51 per cent, five years later, while belief in Christ's resurrection declined from 72 per cent to 42 per cent.

While 98 per cent of students in 2003 said they believed in God, the figure now stands at 94 per cent. The shift is even more striking when it comes to the belief in God as creator, down from 94 per cent to 74 per cent (Peregin 2009). Even faith in things like fortune telling, the horoscope, re-incarnation and the existence of more than one god have dropped dramatically. The authors said this showed a consistency among unbelievers that their lack of belief in the traditional Christian faith is not being replaced by other beliefs or superstition.

Students from the more agrarian island Gozo were more likely to accept the basic tenets of faith than their Maltese counterparts, while female respondents also displayed more faith than males. Sixty per cent of those interviewed said they attended Mass on Sundays or more frequently, a drop of more than 17 per cent compared with 2003. Prayer remained popular among students with 84 per cent saying they pray, compared with 89 per cent in 2003.

> "Religion will not regain its old power until it can face change in the same spirit as does science" (Whitehead)

One-fifth of the respondents agreed with the statement that "faith is more of a dream, which turns out to be an illusion when one is confronted with the harshness of life." A majority of 54 per cent disagreed. Thirty-one per cent said that "in the end, faith is nothing more than a safety net for human fears" and nine per cent went as far as saying that "faith is an expression of a weak personality."

Further, one-third of the students said a scientific understanding of human life and the world made religious understanding superfluous. According to the authors, the study reveals a shift from the traditional structured concept of religion to a broader sense of spirituality. The survey also showed that 57 per cent of the students believed that divorce should be legalised in Malta and 37 per cent said abortion could sometimes be morally acceptable, especially when it came to saving a mother's life or if the child was going to be disabled (Peregin 2009).

This small island depicts the change that modernity coupled with education can bring about. The same will be true in India in a couple of years from now. At the same time, it must be noted that young people are not really turning against religiosity. They are seeking a broader spirituality and more relevant religiosity. Here the words of the famous mathematician-philosopher, Alfred North Whitehead, are relevant: "Religion will not regain its old power until it can face change in the same spirit as does science" (Whitehead 1925).

4

Key Role of Music in Spiritual Life

The popularity of A. R. Rahman's "Jai Ho" urges us to dwell on the profound impact that music has on our spiritual life. Music is not merely unique to humans, but it symbolises the noblest in human life: its enigma, its profundity and spiritual yearning.

Music leads to the mysterious in our existence, to the inexpressible, which relates to what can't be said or said only by allusion, allegory or metaphor. The musical mystery isn't the unutterable, but the ineffable. And the ineffable is not the unsayable, but is inexpressible because there is something to say about it interminably, infinitely: such as the impenetrable mystery of God, or the inexhaustible mystery of love, which is the poetic mystery par excellence.

> Music can take us to realms that are transcendental, religious, mystical and cosmic.

Undeniably, music opens up in us a region where unspoken sentiments can be represented and our being-affected can be expressed. Music expands our emotional space, where there can occur feelings that are absolutely unspoken. When we listen to such music, we enter into a region of the soul which cannot be explored otherwise. Each work is authentically a modality of the soul, a modulation of the soul, as pointed out by the French thinker, Paul Ricoeur.

Ultimately music is the limit case of our language. Most musicians, in fact, are not into language, they are into the organisation of sound. It is, perhaps, the relation between the signified and the sound that is the limit case of our own selves (Ricoeur 1996).

In this way, music can take us to realms that are transcendental, religious, mystical and cosmic. In other words, the expressive, descriptive, allusive power of music enables us to meditate not only on the limits of language but also on its poetic potency! Is music not an expression of the evocative depth of language that gives meaning to human life, or soul to our body?

Very often music creates in us a mood, a feeling, an attitude, a psychological state, which is otherwise not attainable.

The sensation produced by music may be compared with that which is provoked in us by the game of architectural forms. Goethe understood this well when he said, "Architecture is petrified music." If one accepts this thesis that music is a pure sonorous universe, a construction ordained between the human and time, must we not admit that music takes us beyond utilitarian language and, thus, opens us to the sacred space? If so, music is the realm of the most majestic in us!

Music reshapes or refigures or transfigures our world. It helps us to be attuned to life, by placing ourselves in the same tone, co-ordinating tonalities, harmonising, tuning. In singing or listening to music, they are not only actualised, but created, each piece of music engenders its chain of tonalities, its movement of moods, of humours. Such a "refiguration" of both our inner and outer worlds expresses the capacity of music to restructure the world of the listener in "upsetting his horizon, contesting his expectations, remodelling his feelings in reworking them from the inside" (Ricoeur 1996).

The song of birds is a kind of intermediate stage between erratic noise and meaningful sounds. But human music, coupled with pregnant silence, enables us transcend to the divine realm.

So music is the poetry of life. It is creativity, beauty and melody combined in one. It points to and participates in the *sat-cit-ananda* (being-consciousness-bliss).

5

Music: The Most Spiritual Art Form

There was an insightful incident on Christmas day during the Second World War. The German and American soldiers who agreed on a ceasefire on Christmas day were camping on different valleys nearby. All of a sudden the American soldiers heard "Stille Nacht, heilige Nacht" which is the typical German Christmas hymn. Immediately the American soldiers joined their German rivals with "Silent night, holy night," in the same tune and melody. The song bonded them together and fostered a camaraderie that was unimaginable. They celebrated Christmas meaningfully. From the next day onwards, the war continued and they fought on.

Music has a way of lifting us out of ordinary existence into the extraordinary — into spiritual ecstasy. Music has the capacity to take us to another world. It can lift you 'out of ordinary existence, into the extraordinary — into spiritual ecstasy' as claimed by Douglas Todd, of *Vancouver Sun*. Something about music evokes the sacred in even the most irascible, self-avowed atheists. Friedrich Nietzsche, the German atheist thinker, who announced in the 19th century that "God is dead," admitted to being transformed by music. He danced daily, saying it was his "only kind of piety... his 'divine service'."

Music enables us to reflect on the power of harmony and rhythm, whether one is explicitly religious or not.

Every December, churches in Europe are packed with people listening to "Holy Night" and Handel's Messiah and Bach's choirs. Even agnostics listen to them.

Why this love affair with music? It's energising and healing. Ludwig Van Beethoven put it rather mystically: "Music is the mediation between the spiritual and sensual life." Music may be the most accessible and direct means by which humans can experience, imagine and embody the holy. A case can be made that music is the most spiritual art form and the best metaphor for God – and that music may be even a form of divinity itself. Like God is said to be, music is invisible, powerful, intelligent, demanding, calming, ordering and emotionally moving.

Karen Armstrong pleads for the divinity of music in her bestselling new book, *A Case for God* (Armstrong 2009). She holds that to understand religion you should understand music. Music is both rational and non-rational, like religion. It's based on mathematics and cerebral order, but it's also highly emotional. Thus music, like spirituality, operates at the furthest reaches of thought, the limits of reason.

> "The only proof I need that there is a God, is music" (Kurt Vonnegut).

"In music, subjective and objective become one," Armstrong writes. "Every day, music confronts us with a mode of knowledge that defies logical analysis and empirical proof. Hence, all art constantly aspires to the condition of music; so too, at its best, does theology" (Armstrong 2009).

Armstrong says humans should adopt the same attitude to divinity that they take to absorbing music and other forms of art. Religious insight, she says, is only possible "if people cultivate a receptive, listening attitude, not unlike the way we approach art, music or poetry."

Satirical novelist Kurt Vonnegut, who is highly critical of organised religions and rational arguments for God may be right when he holds: "The only proof I need that there is a God, is music" (Seyfried 2010). Listening silently to our own heart beats, we must open ourselves to the divine within and without, so that the soldiers who sang together need not fight against each other the next day.

6

Spirituality Can Help in Times of Recession

Now is the time for recession or depression in the economy as well as in spirituality.

As stock prices go down, people feel its effect on their lives. One has even come across reports of many who have taken their lives because of the economic crisis.

Recent scientific studies show that those who worship a higher power often find solace in times of trouble. Research from Temple University, Philadelphia, US, suggests that a person's religiousness or spirituality can offer some insight into risk of depression. Lead researcher Joanna Maselko characterised the religiosity of 918 study participants in terms of three domains of spirituality — religious service attendance, which refers to being involved with a church; religious well-being, which refers to the quality of a person's relationship with a higher power; and existential well-being, which refers to a person's sense of purpose in life (Temple University 2008).

In a study published in *Psychological Medicine*, Maselko and fellow researchers compared each domain of religiosity with their risk of depression, and were surprised to find that the group with higher levels of religious well-being was 1.5 times more likely to have had depression than the one with lower levels of religious well-being (Temple University 2008). Maselko thinks that this is because people with depression tend to use religion as a coping mechanism. As a result, they're more closely relating to God and praying more. They also found that those who attended religious services were 30 per cent less likely to have had depression in their lifetime, and those who had high levels of existential well-being were 70 per cent less likely to have had depression than those who had low levels of existential well-being.

Involvement in the church provides the opportunity for community interaction, which could help forge attachments to others, an important factor in preventing depression, says Maselko. She stressed that those with higher levels of existential-well being had a strong sense of their place in the world. "People with high levels of existential well-being tend to have a good base, which makes them very centred emotionally," Maselko says. "People who don't have those things are at greater risk for depression, and those same people might also turn to religion to cope" (Temple University 2008).

Maselko admits that researchers are yet to determine which comes first: depression or being religious, but is investigating the time sequence of this over people's lives to figure out the answer. "For doctors, psychiatrists and counsellors, it's hard to disentangle these elements when treating mental illness," she said. "You can't just ask a patient if they go to church to gauge their spirituality or coping behaviours. There are other components to consider when treating patients, and it is important information for doctors to have."

> Genuine spirituality helps us go beyond sorrow and joy

The research shows that spirituality may be of different types, which offer various means of coping with the world. But confronted with depression or despair, spirituality has a significant role to play in helping people cope with such eventualities. So, spirituality does help a patient to deal with his or her difficulties.

At the same time, it must be noted that spirituality cannot be written off when things are bright. A genuine person finds solace and strength in spirituality even when things are flourishing.

Going a step further, one can say that genuine spirituality helps us go beyond sorrow and joy.

7

Doubts are Part of Collective Existence

It is ordinarily understood that a spiritual person believes in God, which casts away all doubt. It is further assumed that a spiritually mature person is certain about her faith. Such a view is often shared by common people who visit gurus to get answers for life's serious problems. The common person assumes that the guru has all the answers since he is somehow in direct contact with the Divine.

We can very well understand the need for safety and security in our day-to-day lives. For instance, a child requires physical and emotional security. The mother or father who provides such a security is the child's deity. In fact, psychologists are aware that a degree of emotional stability and security in childhood is necessary for the sound emotional growth of a human person.

Similarly at the spiritual level, a degree of spiritual certainty and emotional balance is necessary for spiritual growth and flowering. A spiritual child requires such spiritual certainty, which will enable her to mature religiously and innerly.

But as the child grows up, she confronts crucial problems. The child-like certainty, which gave her shelter and kept her going, needs to give rise to a healthy and gradual uncertainty, which borders on openness and doubt.

Great spiritual persons have shown that such a healthy scepticism is indeed the necessary ingredient of their spiritual journey. Buddha refused to give a definitive answer to the questions of life after death.

Mother Teresa lived a life of agonising torture and doubt for years (Ortberg 2008).

The examples of these great persons remind us that although we keep on experiencing the beauty and depth of divinity in our daily lives, there must be room for healthy scepticism. At the deepest spiritual realm there is, and must be, a place for the "darkness of the soul" open to the Unknown and the Unknowable.

> A spiritually deep person is more a question than an answer.

Such a creative scepticism is not atheism or agnosticism as they are commonly expressed. An atheist has either no need of God or claims that God cannot be known. On the other hand, a believer experiences God, knows that God is the most important dimension in her whole life and is even ready to give herself totally to him. At the same time, she is open to further unknowns. All that she cherishes so much, she knows, may give rise to a better or deeper reality.

She has a taste for the Divine, which drives her ahead. And she is sure that she has not reached the destination. So she can remain open to other faith experiences, which may be contradictory to hers.

Such an attitude of healthy scepticism, grounded on an experience of faith, will enable us to explore further. Such an attitude will help us deal with fanaticism and fundamentalism, which has been unfortunately associated with religion.

The need of the hour is to have creative and committed religious persons who have experienced God and who are aware that faith in God does not remove all uncertainties of life. Doubts, ambiguities and questions are necessary part of our collective existence. God has designed the world and humans in such a way that we learn to live with such uncertainties and in this very process become more mature and compassionate. So as religious persons, we are called not only to question our faith in God and our commitment to our fellowhumans, but also to live the very questions we pose. In this sense, a human being is the greatest question to herself. A spiritually deep person is more a question than an answer.

8

Stimulants in Our Spiritual Life

It is a truism to hold that we live on good healthy nourishment. Without healthy and nutritious food we cannot engage ourselves with our daily activities. So, moderate, regular and conscious intake of food is very crucial for a healthy body and a healthy mind. Such food builds us up and enables us to live healthily and function properly. But too much of it or too little of it makes us malfunction.

Together with nourishment, we also need a limited amount of stimulants. Stimulants, as the name implies, stimulates our senses and get us excited and feel "high." Simple foods like coffee and tea are stimulants that make me feel "great," exhilarated and take me out of the daily routine. But the danger with stimulants is that they tend to make us addicted. The law of diminishing returns is true in the case of stimulants. The kick we get with one cup of coffee can be maintained after a few days only with higher amount of caffeine. Not just drugs, drinks and sex, but any addiction over which we have no control and which our body craves for, are stimulants. In the long run stimulants have a capacity to control us and ruin the healthy lifestyle, by making us crave for "kick" without which we cannot maintain our regular life.

What is true at the physical level of nourishment and stimulant is applicable at the intellectual, emotional, social and spiritual level. At the spiritual level too, we need nourishment that enables us to relax, feel at home in the world and be true to ourselves. For that, we definitely need moments of healthy silence, taking care of ourselves, enjoying the daily works and taking time to look into our own selves.

At the spiritual level, we can also have stimulants. A person, who goes after the "spiritual kick" by frequently moving from one guru to another, or by unceasingly making one pilgrimage after another, or by grabbing one book after another, exposes herself to the danger not only of spiritual syncretism, but spiritual flippancy and stimulation. Spiritual stimulants can be as dangerous as physical ones. Someone who is addicted to holy activities like prayer and penance may be unconsciously looking for the "kick" or thrill that such activities provide. That is definitely not a healthy or liberating spirituality.

Genuine spirituality nourishes our whole life, builds it up and enables us to relate to one another in a healthy and gratifying manner. It liberates us so that we can cope with the challenges of life and grapple with its uncertainties. It helps us to realise that in spite of the apparent upheavals and troubles we face, we can be content and joyful deep down, because we are truly at home in the finite world.

> Without being satisfied with easy answers and naïve conclusions, we search consistently and seek to reach the depths of our own being.

Healthy and realistic spirituality nourishes our whole life. Without being satisfied with easy answers and naïve conclusions, it searches consistently and seeks to reach the depths of our own being. Without denying the sufferings and joys of ordinary world, it enables us to be deeply satisfied and fulfilled. Without turning a blind eye to our own weaknesses and failures, it uplifts us and makes us see the noble and good aspects of ourselves and others. Without running away from suffering and pain, we become committed to reducing unnecessary pain and accepting necessary ones without bitterness.

So we need to see to it that religion and spirituality, the most intimate and powerful means of realising ourselves, is protected from becoming a "stimulant" that provides us only with cheap kick or thrill. Religion has to nourish us, make us whole.

9

Scientific Study of Spirituality

India is traditionally proud of being a nation of spiritual seekers. In fact, it is generally assumed that Indians are imbued with a deep sense of spirituality. This is evident when a detached observer watches some of the religious feasts that are celebrated here. People's fervour, devotion and dedication, along with the gaiety and spontaneity, make it evident that spirituality emerges naturally from the depth of an ordinary Indian.

Can such spirituality be scientifically, critically and sympathetically studied? Such a study, if undertaken, is experiential and so different from comparative religions and philosophies.

Sandra Schneiders from the University of Berkeley is a prominent thinker who treats spirituality as an academic subject. She holds that "we are witnessing the prolonged and difficult birth, within the halls of the academy, of a new scholarly discipline called spirituality" (Schneiders 1986).

She compares the study of spirituality to the study of music or fine arts. There are different purposes for the study of music and she holds that one cannot easily decide the primary purpose. The scientific study of music may be either to play a musical instrument better or to develop theoretical knowledge.

Still the question remains: In what way can the academic study of spirituality be connected with lived spirituality? What is the primary purpose of spirituality studies? Can a personally lived spirituality be considered a pre-condition for a critical study of spirituality?

Schneiders makes a distinction between "formation-oriented study" and "research-oriented study."

Her favourite research methodology is the anthropological method, which is inter-disciplinary and inter-religious. Actual spiritual experiences and testimonies can be part of this research method. Schneiders holds that, essentially, the anthropological approach takes as its starting point neither the religious tradition that informs or governs the researcher nor the historical record of spiritual experiences but the spirituality intrinsic to the human subject as such."

Regarding the personal involvement of the researcher, Schneiders says all students she has come upon have used their own spiritual experiences "as a source of question, as analogical data, as comparative resource, as an indicator for validation and falsification." Furthermore, she encourages research students to visit people, who practise a different kind of spirituality than their own. This enables students to use in their research possesses actually lived spiritual experiences – their own as well as those of others – as a "resource for the study of spirituality" (Schneiders 1986).

Schneiders feels that only people, who themselves actually live a spiritual life, can undertake such a research. Nobody who does research in this field can avoid undergoing a transformation in themselves in this process. Nevertheless she claims that research activity cannot have personal change as its primary purpose and that the personal practice should not be an explicit part of most research projects.

Dr. Teresa Peter from the University of Innsbruck, Austria, is an ardent proponent of such a critical study (Peter 2008). She points out the difficulties in integrating spiritual experiences into academic studies. She holds that there is always the danger of one losing the necessary distance needed to do objective scientific research on spirituality.

Still such a scientific and sympathetic study can foster a deeper appreciation of spirituality and purify it from unhealthy deviations and practices.

10

Democratic Spirit and Spirituality

Jaswant Singh's book (Singh 2009), "Jinnah: India-Partition Independence," and the controversy surrounding it points to the power of ideas — rather of free thought — in public space, which is well illustrated in another recently released book, "The Idea of Justice," by Amartya Sen (Sen 2009).

At the heart of Sen's argument is a respect for reasoned differences in our understanding of what a "just society" really is. One of his earliest and most famous claims was that famines do not occur in properly functioning democracies with a free press, because the pressure of public opinion forces the fairer distribution of food.

Democracy, especially in the shape of public argument and debate, plays a key role in Sen's latest work. Public reasoning is the "primary hero" of "The Idea of Justice." It is up to individuals to determine their own course through life, based on their own reasoning and reflection — in this sense, Sen is a liberal — but the tackling of injustice and the shaping of progress rely on a constant, engaged public conversation. For Sen, democracy is not, at heart, a set of institutions and rules. "The working of democratic institutions, like that of all other institutions," he writes, "depends on the activities of human agents."

Elsewhere, Sen narrates what happened to him in the summer of 1997, a time when internet was not widespread. He was asked by a leading Japanese newspaper what he thought was the most important thing that had happened in the 20th century. "I found this to be an unusually thought-provoking question, since so many things of gravity have happened over the last hundred years. The European empires, especially the British and French ones that had so dominated the nineteenth century, came to an end. We witnessed two world wars. We saw the rise and fall of fascism and Nazism. The century witnessed the rise of communism, and its fall (as in the former Soviet Bloc) or radical transformation (as in China)" (Sen 1999).

Sen also recalls the shift from the economic dominance of the west to a new economic balance much more dominated by Japan and East and South-East Asia. Even though that region is going through some financial and economic problems right now, this is not going to nullify the shift in the balance of the world economy that has occurred over many decades (in the case of Japan, through nearly the entire century).

His conclusion: "The past hundred years are not lacking in important events. Nevertheless, among the great variety of developments that have occurred in the twentieth century, I did not, ultimately, have any difficulty in choosing one as the pre-eminent development of the period: the rise of democracy." No democracy can exist without free thinking and writing.

Similar ideas can be traced in his earlier book, *The Argumentative Indian* (Sen 2005). Here, Sen argues for the defence of India's secular politics, the removal of inequalities related to class, caste, gender and community, and the pursuit of sub-continental peace so that democracy succeeds.

"Free press is a great institution in a modern democracy and it has a vital role to play in improving the quality of governance, particularly in a country like ours where channels of communication are still not what they ought to be," Sen writes.

What Sen does in the social sphere is valid in our spiritual realm, too. Without inner freedom, curiosity, open debate, public discourse and a sense of our fairness, spiritual growth will remain stunted.

God and Religion

11

God: Present Everywhere and Nowhere

The disciple wanted to show off a bit and posed the question to the master: "If you can show me a place where God is, I shall give you Rs 1,000." After looking into his eyes, the master retorted, "I shall give you Rs 2,000 if you show me a place where he is not present."

Every believer recognises that God is present everywhere. Still we go to temples and for pilgrimages. We look for special people and places that indicate God's presence to us. We want to experience special events or miracles that show us that God has been extremely kind to us.

This tension between a God who is omnipresent and a God who is concrete, lies, in fact, not in the Divine, but in ourselves. These two aspects constitute the basic human structure.

On the one hand, we are rooted. We are bound, and we are focused. We need close relatives, friends and a stable environment. We need the feeling of closeness and a sense of belonging. We are dependent on our parents, relative and close friends.

Such a God is one I can pray to. Such a God challenges me, inspires me personally and provides me consolation and solace. Such a God is personally involved in my life.

On the other hand, we also need wings that will take us beyond our own comfort zones. We need challenges that will captivate us to soar beyond.

We need visions and dreams that will take us beyond the chains that bind us. The God of ordinary people, including the famous scientist-philosopher, Blasé Pascal, represents such a God.

This God, at times derogatively referred to as "the God of philosophers," provides us with categories and frames of references. This God is the God of the universe, the creator and sustainer of it. He is the source of all mystery, power and cosmic abundance. This is the Cosmic Power found in Albert Einstein's mystical experience.

> God "whose centre is everywhere and circumference is nowhere"

So, as human beings, we live between our universal or cosmic feelings and the concrete or particular needs. It is only when we can deal with both these aspects, can we be fully human.

Similarly, in our religious or spiritual life, we have a God who is close to us, who is interested in us and who stands by us. Such a God is interested in our personal welfare and is involved in our failures and success. A God who "calls us by name" and who cares for "even the hair on our head."

But we also have a God who is interested in the whole universe, including our enemies and rivals. A God, compassionate to everyone. A God who is not just focused on our little world, but is present everywhere.

On the one hand, I need a God who is concerned about me and who looks at me with love and understanding, who looks at my face tenderly.

On the other, we also need a God "whose centre is everywhere and circumference is nowhere" as Middle Age thinkers used to say.[2] A God, who dwells in the "cave of my heart."

12

To Be Religious Is to Be Inter-Religious

Recently, there were reports that Europe was becoming sensitive to the rising presence of Islam. The latest dispute is in Switzerland, acclaimed for its harmonious living and scenic beauty. Switzerland is planning a referendum to ban minarets on mosques. Similarly, Italy's interior minister vowed to close a controversial mosque in Milan.[3]

The fear of many Europeans is that Muslims aren't assimilating, and not accepting western values, posing a threat to security. "It's a visible symbol of anti-Muslim feelings in Europe," says Danièle Joly, director of Center for Research in Ethnic Relations at the University of Warwick in England. Many in Europe are feeling threatened by the Muslims. The disputes reflect unease with the estimated 18 million Muslims who constitute the continent's second-biggest religion, living among Western Europe's predominantly Christian population of 400 million.

In this background, I want to reflect on our Indian experience of living in a multi-religious environment.

It is insightful to note what Arnold Toynbee, the British historian, has to say about India: "It is already becoming clear that a chapter which had a Western beginning will have to have an Indian ending if it is not to end in the self-destruction of the human race. At this supremely dangerous moment in history, the only way of salvation for mankind is the Indian way."

I believe that India has an inspiring lesson to teach the larger world with regard to true inter-religious encounter. Though India is predominantly a Hindu nation, it has the second largest Muslim population in the world. In spite of occasional tensions and conflicts, overall, India has maintained a healthy and creative relationship between various religious communities.

Indians are proud of the fact that four of the world's living religions, besides the various tribal religions, originated here. It is a remarkable feat that in spite of the multiplicity of religions and conflicting world views, we have been able to interact with each other and in the process deepen each other's spiritual insights.

Spiritual people, like the Buddha, Asoka, Gandhi and Mother Teresa, are symbols of Indian ethos where deep religiosity leads to respect for and learning from each other. Though "argumentative Indians" do assert their views, there is a deep respect for each other. India is a place where diversity is respectfully affirmed and celebrated.

What is significant is that such tolerance between religions stems not because of any indifference, but from a deep-rootedness in one's own and openness to others' religious traditions.

Just as Islam has become part of India, the larger world has to learn to respect all religious traditions, including atheism, with love for each other. Only such a respectful dialogue can save us from the "conflict of civilisations" that some thinkers like to speak of. Such a "conflict" leads to our own destruction and cannot come from the depth of a spiritual person. The Indian experience teaches us that in today's world "to be religious is to be inter-religious." An authentically religious person ought to live with and learn from other religious traditions.

We can agree with the American philosopher, Will Durant: "India will teach us the tolerance and gentleness of a mature mind, understanding spirit and a unifying, pacifying love for all human beings."[4]

13

Religion: Without God?

Richard Dawkins, in his book, "The God Delusion," has described pantheism as "sexed-up atheism." Though this term seems flippant, it is close to pantheism.

What's the difference between atheism and pantheism? As far as disbelief in supernatural beings, forces or realms, is concerned, there is no difference. Pantheism also shares the respect for evidence, science and logic, feelings typical of atheism.

According to a website on pantheism, it adds to atheism an embracing, positive and reverential feeling about our lives on planet earth, our place in nature and the wider universe, and uses nature as our basis for dealing with stress, grief and bereavement. It's a form of spirituality that is compatible with science. Indeed, since science is our best way of exploring the universe, respect for the scientific method and fascination with the discoveries of science are an integral part of world pantheism.

According to these groups, if atheism, humanism and naturalism are to progress, then they need approaches that do not simply leave the individual alone in the face of an increasingly threatening physical, social and international environment. They need ways of life that offer as rich a range of benefits as traditional religious ones.

A growing number of people declare themselves to be non-religious or atheists. The proof is in bestseller books by atheist authors such as Dawkins, Sam Harris and Christopher Hitchens. But, so far atheism and atheist groups have focused on attacking conventional religions, especially Judaism, Christianity and Islam. In many cases, they give credence to backward, repressive or destructive social values, developed in agrarian societies.

But, according to some of these thinkers, negative critiques will not suffice. There are many motives beyond fear or habit as to why people hold on to old religions or convert to new ones. There are many reasons besides ignorance and folly why they make religion the centre of their personal and social lives.

Religions are not just a confidence trick on the part of prophets and preachers, or a self-destructive aberration on the part of believers. They have had social survival value in the past, and continue to provide individual and personal benefits today. Religions provide communities with mutual support. They overcome existential isolation and alienation, giving people a meaning for their lives and a sense of their place in the universe and nature. Moreover, they combat the feeling of helplessness in a threatening world full of crime, conflict and disaster. These benefits show up in the form of better health and longer life, as some atheists themselves admit.

Are these negatives an inevitable part of the bargain? They may well be an inevitable part of belief in the unbelievable or of uncritical adherence to ancient scriptures. Is it impossible to get the benefits that conventional religions offer, without giving up the advantages offered by science and atheism? Don't we need approaches that offer the same range of advantages as supernatural religions – but without the costs?

Historically, there could be religion without God, or religious atheism. Buddhism does not have gods. Nor does Taoism of Lao Tzu. Can there be such a thing as a completely natural form of "spirituality" with no supernatural elements? Can human beings find meaning and significance with no Gods, with no transcendence? My conviction is, no.

Can there be such a thing as a completely natural form of "spirituality" with no supernatural elements?

14

Religion: Transformation and Transcendence

By expanding and deepening the way we understand religion and its functions, we can examine religious institutions and spiritual phenomena in a more productive way. Philip Goldberg in "The Huffington Post" proposes a model of religion with the following five functions:[5]

1. Transmission: to impart to each generation a sense of identity through shared customs, rituals, stories, and historical continuity. 2. Translation: to help individuals to interpret life events, acquire a sense of meaning and purpose, and understand their relationship to a larger whole (in both the social and cosmic senses). 3. Transaction: to create and sustain healthy communities and provide guidelines for moral behaviour and ethical relationships.

Further, two less emphasised functions of religion are: 4. Transformation: to foster maturation and ongoing growth, helping people to become more fulfilled and more complete. 5. Transcendence: to satisfy the longing to expand the perceived boundaries of the self, become more aware of the sacred aspect of life, and experience union with the ultimate ground of Being.

Among other things, the above view helps explain why people choose to stay involved with a religion even when they don't fully approve of the institutions they belong to and don't believe all of their traditions' truth claims. Staying religiously engaged connects them to both an ancient heritage and a living community; helps them to comprehend at least some of the mysteries of existence; and gives them some guidelines to live by.

That applies mainly to the first three functions, which are the ones that we tend to think about when we talk about religion. But adding the last two functions to the discussion expands the perspective radically. It also explains a great deal of contemporary spirituality.

For better or worse, organized religions in the West have emphasized the first three functions. But they have, historically, failed to provide opportunities for authentic transformation and transcendence, which accounts for the rise of an entirely new religious category: spiritual but not religious.

The yearning for transformation and transcendence also explains the burgeoning interest in long-hidden mystical teachings. But perhaps the most significant phenomenon driven by the absence of transformation and transcendence in mainstream religion has been the explosion of interest in Eastern traditions. What started with spiritually adventurous baby boomers in the sixties and seventies has since affected tens of millions of people who engage in practices that were, for centuries, the exclusive domain of Hindus, Buddhists, and, to a lesser extent, Taoists. Elements of those traditions were translated and packaged for Western consumption, offering practical methods for transformation and transcendence that did not go against reason, science, or history. Experience-oriented more than belief-oriented, they were adapted for use by people of all faiths – and no faith – who were willing to follow the instruction manuals. This led to the secularization of traditional spiritual practices such as meditation and yoga, and to a remarkable scientific enterprise that has already produced thousands of studies documenting the effectiveness of those disciplines for mental and physical health.

Adding the dimensions of transformation and transcendence helps us do justice to the original purpose of religion: to expand and deepen our sense of ourselves, and to forge a connection to the transcendent. Since the word "religion," derived from the Latin *religare*, which means to bind, we can assess any expression of religion, by how well it binds us to our higher nature, to each other, to the planet, and to the cosmos. Does it bind us enough to make us truly feel at home in this universe? "To the extent that religion fails at those tasks," asserts Goldberg, "it does not live up to its name."

15

Spirituality Without Religion?

Twenty years ago, religion and spirituality were synonymous. One would never have thought of separating the two. Today, however, particularly among young adults, influenced by the New Age Movements, there is a prevailing desire to be spiritual but at the same time a tendency to reject organised religion. "I'm spiritual, but I'm not religious."

Some people believe in God but don't see the need for the structure and rituals of the organised religion. Others believe in a "godly being," perhaps sensing strong feelings of the divine without relating to the institution of religion.

While labelling themselves spiritual, anti-religion advocates will reject the rituals of organised religious institutions, view religion in the context of exclusion (an in-group vs. an out-group), and do not like being preached to or having rules imposed upon them. Espousing individualism and finding their own identity, they reject religion because they see the institutional religion as assigning their identity. So, they shape their own spirituality like consumers going to the supermarket with many options available to them, choosing what they want and disregarding what they find unappealing.

"What a lot of people are saying in that phrase is that spirituality is personal and religion is communal. They feel very comfortable sharing their spiritual identity because it's something they get to create for themselves. They will say, 'my spirituality is mine and I can put it together any way that makes sense to me. I can make it what

I want it to be.'" The missing element in this kind of spirituality is community. "Religion is not all about you. It's also about other people. When I say I am religious, I don't get to determine it, and I don't get to make up the rules. They were given to me, handed down to me," said a Canadian Catholic Archbishop Gerard Pettipas. A person claiming to be spiritual but not religious is akin to somebody saying he favours education but does not like schools, he said.

The non-religious spiritual persons do not want their self-made spirituality impacting their behaviour and how they choose to live their lives. They try to be good people, relative to their own belief systems. Speaking as they would, he said, "I am happy to say that I am spiritual. I am happy to say that I recognise something beyond the physical world. I am happy to say that I have a connection with not just the divine, but also with other people, and that those connections have an impact on my life." Religion, thus, provides values and virtues to a group and makes life viable leading to a meaningful spirituality.

Religion provides values and virtues to a group and makes life viable leading to a meaningful spirituality.

At the same time the sense of despondency and rejection many people feel against organised religions is a clarion call that religions have to take seriously. As Max Weber, through the dilemma of institutionalisation, reminds us: for a religion to survive structures of authority are necessary. But these structures of authority, meant to propagate the spiritual vision, can become self-directed and selfish. In such a situation, religion becomes a hindrance to true spirituality. So, there is always a need for organised religion to discern in order to correct itself. Just as individuals cannot claim to be spiritual without being religious, religions cannot claim to be religious and so spiritual. The relationship between them is much more complex and nuanced. So we need to be open to the Divine that is both in our own hearts as well as in the face of the "Other."

16

Religious Leaders: Can They Handle Power?

Recently, a few Christian and Hindu religious leaders were in the news for the wrong reasons. I am not going to make any judgment on their actions. At the same time, I wish to reflect on religious leadership and the presence of evil in everyone's heart.

Religion is primarily there to foster goodness and reduce evil in the world. The primary role of religion is to reduce suffering and evil. At the same time, historians of religions remind us of the truth of the axiom, "Power corrupts, absolute power corrupts absolutely."

We must acknowledge that religion, like all other human organisations, strives to improve the human condition. Like all other organisations, religious leaders too fail at times. They too are prone to sin and corruption. When they acquire power there is the inherent danger that they may feel "superior" to others and hence use them for their own personal advantage.

Spiritual power is all embracing, since the spiritual realm embraces the whole of human life. So the power religious leaders exercise is more personal, intimate and all embracing. When religious leaders fail, it has terrible consequences, devastating many more human lives, than political or social leaders.

When we reflect on human life, post-modernists remind us that every human action involves power. Starting from the gentle touch of a mother, we are always involved in the exchange of power. Most of the time, this power is positive and liberating. At times, the power may become dehumanising and even demonic. This is true of our material and social existence. War and violence, exploitation and enslavement of human beings can be understood thus.

Unfortunately, this is also true of the religious and spiritual realm. A genuinely spiritual person experiences the vacuum or emptiness within and depends totally on the power of God. For such a person, the only source of power is God, which he tries to share with others. A genuine leader is not influenced by the applause of his followers or the prestige that comes from his success.

A true mystic is one who has discovered the powerlessness within and who has accepted it. If one accepts the "nothingness" from within, then one does not need to fill that "nothingness" from outside. Such leaders are totally dependent on God, who alone can fill their inner vacuum. Paradoxically, when such mystics truly realise their own inner emptiness and accept it, they are filled with joy and love. For such a person, the acceptance of inner emptiness is truly a source of the abundance of life.

Unlike such genuine leaders, most of us try to fill our emptiness with external things. Money, sex, pleasures and even power become a means to fill the emptiness. The worst form of abuse of power is the power over people. If religious leaders use their followers in order to fill their own inner emptiness, that becomes a ready recipe for exploiting the hapless victims.

So the challenge before religions is to form leaders who are comfortable with their own emptiness. Such leaders will be comfortable with silence: silence of words, actions and even thoughts. They will also be comfortable with their own inadequacies and failures, without the need to justify their frailties. They will know that it is much better to suffer than inflict pain on others. Such people will be self-disciplined. They alone can confront evil, without fostering it directly or indirectly.

17

Religion: Challenge and Criticism

"Religulous" is a funny and thought-provoking documentary recently released in the US. In that documentary, the comedian and outspoken non-believer Bill Maher travels the world, interviewing Christians, Jews and Muslims, critiquing religions.

Early on in the documentary, Religulous, the political commentator Bill Maher states his thesis: "Religion is detrimental to humanity." He is seen hopping around the world, trying to prove this with various interviews and comments (Krishnamurti 1956; PennLive 2008).

His quest, for instance, takes him to Orlando, where he asks an actor, who plays Jesus, "Why do you think people come here? Because Disneyland is too smutty?" He goes to Miami's Growing in Grace Ministry, where he meets its founder, Jose Luis de Jesus Miranda, who has gotten rich claiming to be Jesus Christ returned (Rodriguez 2008).

His journey takes him to London and Amsterdam meeting Christians, Jews and Muslims, making fun of them. He does not even spare scientologists and Mormons. He sits down with many similar religious groups, pointing out their idiosyncrasies.

Throughout Religulous, unfortunately, Maher focuses too much on entertainment, which will frustrate viewers expecting a deeper, more satisfying exploration of the film's subject. It doesn't require a lot of ingenuity to point out the absurdity of religious fundamentalism of any kind, something Religulous does very effectively. It's a lot harder to explore the point at which scientific thought must or may give way to spiritual depth.

Occasionally, the documentary gives us people worthy of its ambitious subject matter, like Maher's interview with Father Reginald Foster, a senior Vatican scholar with a surprisingly progressive view of Catholicism, or Francis Collins, the highly respected geneticist, also a practising Christian. In scenes like those, Religulous challenges our notions about institutional science and religion, finding a fascinating grey area in a territory that's almost always seen as either/or.

> "The religion that is afraid of science, dishonours God and commits suicide." R. W. Emerson

But the bulk of the film is a passionate but misguided attempt by Maher to stimulate 16 per cent of the American population who regard themselves as atheist to stand up. Maher, born to a Jewish mother and raised as a Christian, considers himself an agnostic. He sums up his vision: "Religion must die for mankind to live!" (PennLive 2008).

Although Maher does not in any way relate to the Indian scene, he still helps us indirectly realise the idiosyncrasies in our own religions. In this way, it helps us to purify ourselves individually and challenge ourselves collectively.

Further, such critiques do not necessarily make us defensive. Instead, we know that only when we are challenged from outside, can we truly mature. Critiques, such as Religulous enable us to look into our own spirituality more critically and come up with creative responses. Only such religions can cope with the modern contours of life.

Spirituality or religion do have direct implications for both our interior and external behaviour. Besides the interior freedom that religion offers, it inevitably helps us to be externally committed. A religion that does not positively contribute to the well-being of fellow human beings is not worth following.

That is why more than 150 years ago, American philosopher Ralph Waldo Emerson said: "The religion that is afraid of science, dishonours God and commits suicide" (Walls 2003).[6]

18

Religion Enhances Our Commitment

We are confronted by dangers and crises, needing both short-term and long-term responses. Unfortunately, our biological evolution has made us adept at handling short-term crises and not long-term ones. Many of contemporary problems could be traced to such a disparity in responding to crises and investing time for solving them.

As reported recently in "The New York Times," Professor Daniel Gilbert argues that the threats that get our attention tend to have four features. First, they are personalised and intentional. The brain is highly evolved for social behaviour and, like gazelles, we are always on the lookout for enemies (Kristof 2009).

Second, we respond to threats that we deem explicitly disgusting or immoral — characteristics more associated with sex, betrayal or spoiled food than with atmospheric chemistry. He explains: "That's why people are incensed about flag burning, or about what kind of sex people have in private, even though that doesn't really affect the rest of us. Yet where we have a real threat to our well-being, like global warming, it doesn't ring alarm bells" (Kristof 2009).

Third, threats get our attention when they are imminent, while our brain circuitry is often indifferent about the future. Economists are puzzled by our irrational behaviour called hyperbolic discounting: people's preference for money now rather than much larger payments later. For example, in studies, most people prefer to opt for Rs 1,000 now to rather than Rs 2,000 in six months, even though that represents a 100 per cent increase.

Fourth, we're far more sensitive to changes that are instantaneous than those that are gradual. We care the least about the slow melting of glaciers, while if there is a collapsed house in our neighbourhood, we respond immediately.

We're brilliantly programmed to act on the risks that confronted us in the Pleistocene Age. We're less adept with 21st century challenges that threaten our collective existence. It is here that a considered religious way of life can lend a hand to cope with both our short-term and long-term crisis. Religion not only enables us to "postpone the gratification of our needs" for a joyous life after death, but also helps us for rigorous and sustained commitment. The huge problems we face need planning and response that are both short term and long term. We need sustained and even unnoticed effort to see ourselves through.

In fact, authentic religion is not about the next world, but primarily about this world. It will help us to use crises for our collective enhancement. Such a religion is neither obscurantist, nor dogmatic, but the source of energy and hope for sustained commitment even for long-term goals. Further, religious fervour facilitates us to seek beyond our individual goals to search for collective fulfilment. Thus religion helps us to transcend our narrow myopic vision, opening us to the larger issues confronting us collectively. The insight of the British historian, Arnold Toynbee, is valid even for us: "We have been God-like in our planned breeding of our domesticated plants and animals, but we have been rabbit-like in our unplanned breeding of ourselves" (McDonald 2004). Spirituality and religion, coupled with scientific insights and technological prowess, can truly help us to face the short-term and long-term challenges and crises confronting us and respond adequately. Only thus can we adequately respond to the larger issues — social, economic, political and religious — of our century.

19

God: Beyond Propitiation

Recently a five-year-old Indian girl died after holy men advised a group to perform a torture-ritual on her in the hope of finding a treasure. Three days later, the police found the child's body near a dam, nearly two miles away from her village in Maharashtra. A post-mortem revealed that she had suffered multiple injuries.

"She had been physically tortured. Her hair had been pulled out. We suspected some sacrificial ritual and questioned two tantriks," the police said. One of them allegedly told the others that a treasure was buried underneath a tamarind tree near their village. To get to the treasure, they had to perform a ritual ceremony on a young girl. "A puja must be performed on a young girl to get this wealth," they were informed. So they abducted the child, tortured and killed her while performing the ritual.[7]

Such heinous crimes have been perpetuated in one form or other by religious people. Superstitious beliefs of this sort are rampant even among devout and contemporary religious believers. The borderline between genuine faith and harmful superstition is, unfortunately, very thin.

In the course of history, animal and human sacrifices had taken place and, sometimes, even justified. Behind such drastic action is the notion of a god who has to be propitiated. A god who rewards and punishes, depending on whether people appease him or not. A god who needs to be pacified even with human blood!

Given the uncertainties and ambiguities of life, it is tempting to think of a god with his own whims and fancies. Such a god needs offering and sacrifices so that he does not harm us. Such gods, like our malevolent tyrants, seek our obeisance. Their self-esteem is so weak that only our blind submission, it seems, makes them secure and so they crave for it.

In such a world, it makes sense to propitiate gods who, otherwise, will be vicious. But genuine mystics and religious thinkers realise that god wishes only the good of human beings. Anything that hinders human well-being and makes them subservient, goes against basic religious tenets. Any act of propitiation or submissive obeisance is superstition. True religion fosters humble submission to God, not abject submissiveness. It acknowledges the gentle power of God, not the capricious might of a tyrant. It nurtures a healthy relationship between God and humans, which leads to respectful dealings among humans. Anything that endangers human relationship and self-respect is superstitious.

In a genuinely spiritual world, there is never a need for human sacrifice, only for self-sacrifice and self-denial. Just as we need discipline and regularity to be a success in life, we need sacrifice coupled with flexibility and creativity to grow in spiritual life. Growth in spiritual life demands consistent hard work, careful planning and categorical submission to a higher power. None, not even religious leaders, have a right to demand sacrifice from others in the name of God. Therefore, contemporary sensibilities demand that we go beyond a god of propitiation. That is part of humanity's religious growth in religious consciousness.

But since religions are powerful and life-giving, it is easy for even healthy religious practices to become dangerous superstitions. Believers must be extra careful not to let their religious duties become dehumanised. Any religion that doesn't realise this and acts decisively against it, does not deserve to survive.

20

Rationalism: Friend or Foe of Religion

The Guardian reported on March 2010 about a fake Indian guru. A famous tantric boasted on Indian television that he could kill another man using only his mystical powers. While most viewers either gasped in awe or merely nodded unquestioningly, Sanal Edamaruku, the head of the Indian Rationalist Association, challenged him directly: "Go on then - kill me" (Edamaruku 2010).

At first, the holy man was reluctant, but eventually agreed to perform a series of rituals designed to kill Edamaruku live on television. Millions tuned in as the channel cancelled scheduled programming to continue broadcasting the showdown. First, the guru chanted mantras, and then he sprinkled water on his intended victim. He brandished a knife, ruffled the sceptic's hair and pressed his temples. But after several hours of similar antics, Edamaruku was still very much alive – even smiling and taunting the furious holy man.

Edamaruku has dedicated his life to exposing the charlatans — from levitating village fakirs to televangelist yoga masters — who he says are obstructing Indian Enlightenment. "The immediate goal I have is to stop these fraudulent babas and gurus," the part-time journalist and publisher says, "I want people to make their own decisions. They should not be guided by ignorance, but by knowledge. I'd like to see a post-religious society — that would be an ideal dream, but I don't know how long it would take" (Edamaruku 2010).

One common trick he exposes is levitation, usually done using an accomplice who lies on the ground under a blanket and then raises his upper body while holding out two hockey sticks under the blanket to make it look like his feet are also rising. "It's quite easy really," asserts Edamaruku, who teaches members to perform the tricks in villages and then explains how they are done, or demonstrates them at press conferences.

> "A religion that fears reason is an affront to God."

Other simple tricks include walking on hot coals (the skin does not burn if you walk fast enough) and lying on a bed of nails (your weight is spread evenly across the bed). The "weeping statue" trick is usually done by melting a thin layer of wax covering a small deposit of water.

Some tricks require closer scrutiny. One guru in Andhra Pradesh used to boil a pot of tea using a small fire on his head. The secret was to place a non-conductive pad made of compacted wheat flour between his head and the fire. "I was so excited when I exposed him. I should have been more reasonable but sometimes you get so angry," Edamaruku said. "I cried," "Look, even I can do this and I'm not a baba — I'm a rationalist!"

When the television guru's initial efforts to kill him failed, he accused Edamaruku of praying to gods to protect him. "No, I'm an atheist," he emphasised. The holy man then said he needed to conduct a ritual that could only be done at night, outdoors, and after he had slept with a woman, drunk alcohol and rubbed himself in ash. The men agreed to go to an outdoor studio that night - all to no avail. At midnight, the anchor declared the contest is over. Reason had prevailed.

I hold firmly that true religion can only flourish when reason triumphs over gullibility and ignorance. True religion should be tested every day in the crucible of reason and of action. In fact charlatans who exploit the gullibility of the masses are enemies of God and religion. Truly, "A religion that fears reason is an affront to God."

Humans and Body

21

Human Beings: Hardwired for God?

Advances in neuroscience are challenging our traditional ideas about God, religion and the concept of self. Some religious thinkers like to speak of a "God module" and propose a new discipline "neurotheology" and "spiritual neuroscience," which studies mutually the symbiotic relationship between neuroscience and God experience.

Scholars have long speculated that religious feeling can be tied to a specific place in the brain. In his new book, Phantoms in the Brain, noted neurologist V. S. Ramachandran explores "human nature and the architecture of the mind," drawing on examples of the intensely felt (and sometimes bizarre) alterations in behaviour and perception that can arise from injuries and illnesses of the brain.

As noted by Chris Floyd of Science and Spirit, the chapter devoted to the intense religious experiences associated with some types of temporal lobe epilepsy has aroused widespread interest (Floyd 1999). Some religious leaders, for instance, claim that Ramachandran has found an "antenna" in the temporal lobes for receiving the presence of God. At the same time, atheists have also seized on the same research as "proof" that "spiritual experience" is just a misinterpreted tickling in the brainpans and nothing more.

Some of the most fascinating research being done at Ramachandran's centre involves brain injuries and ailments. So he devotes much attention to these cases: amputees suffering from "phantom limbs" — the persistent, often painful experiencing of limbs that have been removed (and the often strenuous efforts to deny the loss); or, conversely, brain-damaged patients who fail to recognise their own existing limbs. Then there are the patients who suddenly can't recognise faces, or who feel their loved ones are "impostors," or who have lost the ability to form new memories, and so on.

Ramachandran also ventures into what he calls "my most speculative theory." "There may be certain neural pathways — neural structures in the temporal lobe and the limbic system — whose activity makes you more prone to religious belief. Now why this would happen, I don't know. One possibility — and this is very speculative — is that human beings are hard-wired for religious beliefs" (Floyd 1999).

"But what's interesting to me in this research is that aspects of human nature that until now were considered inaccessible to scientific investigation — such as religious belief, art, humour — are now open for study. We can at least begin to think about these issues that once remained solely the province of philosophers and theologians."

"But none of this in any way detracts from the value of religious experience," he adds quickly. "Religious experience is a very important part of human nature, and it's completely ignored by scientists. It's one thing to debate whether God exists or not. You can't approach God scientifically. But we can approach religious experience scientifically, and ask which parts of the brain are involved."

"It's that sense of awe and wonder that more than anything else prompts you to believe in God."

Ramachandran believes that science and religion deal with "completely different aspects of human experience," but they are unified in the wonder we experience at the workings of the universe and the brain. "It's that sense of awe and wonder that more than anything else prompts you to believe in God."

22

People: Source and Resource

Many management studies have indicated that human beings themselves can be used as a resource. This is derived from the insight that human capabilities and potential may be, in fact, better resources than natural raw materials, which were traditionally regarded as resources for productivity.

Wikipedia defines human resource management as "the strategic and coherent approach to the management of an organisation's most valued assets — the people working there who individually and collectively contribute to the achievement of the objectives of the business." In management studies today, the terms "human resource management" and "human resources" have largely replaced the term "personnel management." But we need to go further and cherish the singularity, uniqueness and worth of each individual, which may be understood in terms of human beings as a source.

The 5th century BC Attic philosopher Protagoras proposed that "man is the measure of all things" (Russell 2009).[8] But it would imply that in our known world, human beings are the source of all values. The noble virtues like goodness, truth and beauty may not have originated from humans, but they are to be treated differently from things and objects in this world.

Immanuel Kant would hold that "man is an end in himself" and should "never be treated merely as means." According to him, the uniqueness and dignity of human beings are unparalleled compared with things and objects. Martin Buber, a Jewish philosopher, speaks of humans beings as "subjects" capable of entering into I-Thou relationships, while others are "objects" with I-It relationships. Gabriel Marcel regards human beings being basically a "mystery," while non-humans fall under the category of "problems."

Because of the freedom and ability to enter into meaningful relationships, human beings have a unique responsibility to treat each other with dignity. In this sense, they are the source of all values, visions and create collectively their own world.

That is why we treat weak and aged people differently from animals. Without in any way lowering the dignity of other species of living forms, we do realise that we have a higher or even nobler obligation to each other. Our ethics follow from this basic self-understanding of our own special dignity.

Even companies are beginning to realise that people can't be treated merely as means or as functional objects. Pragmatically it is all right at times to use human capabilities for the collective efficiency and betterment of the organisation. But in the long run, the worth and value of each individual has to be affirmed, respected and fostered.

That is a reason why in the management circles, they prefer the term, "human potential management," which focuses on self-management based on the belief, if individuals are respected and provided with opportunities, they could manage themselves better. Recognising their potential, human potential management attempts to enhance human capabilities and capacities through integrative and continuous processes. By achieving their full potential, employees are urged to contribute their best and, in the process, individuals are cherished and their personality respected. Thus human beings are both source and resource, personally and collectively.

23

Mid-Life: The Truth of Myself

In the life of most of us, a time comes when we realise more deeply the sobering and, at times, the painful truth about ourselves. For some, it may be a shattering experience of sickness or death of a beloved. It could also be an encounter with a devastating failure. For others, it could be a joyful or successful event that radically relativises values and changes the direction of life.

Mostly, such radical change happens in the middle age, when we reflect on our own achievements and failures and realise the futility of some of them and the greatness of others. Many of our works and achievements that gave meaning and purpose to our life may cease to be relevant to us. Many of our values become questionable to ourselves. This mid-life crisis is, in fact, a call to come home to the truth of myself.

The mid-life challenge is a wake-up call, reminding me that my achievements might have been at the cost of something more precious. For example, a successful manager may realise that his fame and success has come at the cost of his family happiness. Such an inner call helps to shatter the pseudo well-being that I have developed for myself in the long process of coping with my own life.

As a genuine person I am called to become aware of the truth of myself non-judgmentally and non-violently. The truth about myself is related to my own shadows, unfinished businesses, projections, boundaries and partial perceptions. It also includes the disowned or underdeveloped aspects of my life as well as the polarities and paradoxes of my life. After having become aware of the truth of myself, I am challenged to own it up courageously. This implies that many of my failures or weaknesses are affirmed courageously and accepted peacefully.

This enables me to work through the truth of myself non-violently. This may include the ability to change myself, particularly with regard to the underdeveloped aspects of my life. For instance, someone who has been authoritative and strong throughout his life may discover the need to cultivate compassion and understanding, or someone who has been involved with social work may learn to appreciate the value of silence or vice-versa. While working through the truth of myself, I do not need to force myself or strain myself. Being genuinely aware of myself is, in itself, transformative. As such, being truly aware of my weakness is the beginning of change.

As a result of my awareness and working through the truth of myself, I will have a revisioning of myself and the world. This will result in reorienting the patterns of my behaviour and truly reconciling myself to the truth of my being. Thus, mid-life provides a chance to relativise many of my visions, to reorient myself and to gain new perspectives. Such revisions and perspectives help me to integrate myself with the process of living and finding meaning in my life and relationships. According to Dr Joe Parakad, Director, Sadhana Institute, Lonavla, "Coming home to the truth of myself is the call and challenge of mid-life, which many Indians are only now beginning to appreciate." He adds: "Unless we turn around and gracefully embrace our shadows, they will overtake us and take charge of us."

"Unless we turn around and gracefully embrace our shadows, they will overtake us and take charge of us."
Parakad

Thus, mid-life is a precious and precarious invitation to us. Having relativised my values, broken through my pseudo sense of well-being, mid-life crisis challenges me to own up myself and integrate myself, enabling me to flow effortlessly and joyfully in the ongoing process of life.

24

Loved, Accepted in Our Vulnerability

Everyone wants to be great. To be great is to be appreciated, admired and also imitated. We have great heroes or idols that we wish to follow. We acknowledge the great contribution that these great leaders have made and we are elated by thinking of them. We wish to recognise their greatness and make it our own.

This is a human tendency that begins right from childhood. Psychologists tell us that there is need for children to have "significant others" who will influence and shape them. As a child, we are prone to imitate the actions and even mannerism of our great teachers or acknowledged heroes. This is one way of socialising ourselves into society.

But there is a negative side to the admiration we feel for others. However great they are, however noble their aspirations may be, there is something in us that tells us that they are different from us. On our own, we are finite, weak and broken. So, though we look up to them for inspiration, strength and guidance, there is another aspect that tells us that we will never become as great as they are. The great heroes we idealise are almost "superhumans" who do not have the sense of mortal pain that we, ordinary mortals, feel in our flesh and blood (Waters 2006).

They are elevated to a high pedestal, so we are aware that we can never reach their greatness. "We are too human for it," we console ourselves. Thus along with the admiration we feel for their great achievements, there creeps in a tinge of envy and sadness. For, we will never be like them, however hard we try.

On the other hand, we also look around and see people who are as weak, as fragile and as broken as we are. At the same time most of us keep to ourselves our own brokenness and frailties. Considering them as our weakness to be avoided or at least hidden, we spend quite a lot of our time pretending that they do not exist. We invest so much of our energy to present ourselves as perfect, though deep down most of us know that we are sinful, selfish and cowardly, like most of the human beings around us.

> "In our greatness we are admired, in our vulnerability we are loved"

Definitely, at times there come moments, when I reveal myself in my weakness and vulnerability. Rarely comes a time when I can truly be myself in the company of another, who is as inadequate as I am. When we drop our guards, we reveal our own weakness to the one next to us. The wonder is that most of the time, when we admit our own weakness, we are accepted for what we are. Obviously, it is a risky enterprise. Sometimes when we reveal our inner struggle, we are rejected and left alone.

In fact, these moments, when we reveal our weakness and are accepted for what we are, are truly moments of grace. It is precisely then we feel collectively the depth and vulnerability of being human. It is then that we realise that many others share our fears and go through life with so many imperfections. It is precisely at these moments that we are accepted, affirmed and so transformed. It is a moment of love.

A lover is one, to whom I can reveal everything and feel totally comfortable. A lover is one from whom I do not need to hide anything, in order to be accepted. To a lover I can reveal my deepest fears and deadliest sins.

So "in our greatness we are admired, in our vulnerability we are loved," as Dr Parakad of Sadhana Institute is fond of repeating.

25

Power and the Weaker Sex

According to a scientific study conducted in Israel and circulated world-wide, men are, in fact, the "weaker sex." In his research of 66,000 births at Israel's Rabin Medical Centre between 1995 and 2006, Prof Marek Glezerman found that males were more likely to develop complications during birth. Surprisingly, he found that this vulnerability continued throughout boys' adulthood (Leach 2009).

"Men are known to have a shorter life span, are more susceptible to infections and have less chance of withstanding a disease than women. In short, men are the weaker sex," concluded Professor Glezerman.

According to another researcher, Jennifer Graves of the Australian National University, males are more susceptible to greater risks in the post-natal period and "are more likely to expose themselves to risky behaviour later in life." Comparing the male and female species, she was very emphatic: "It's almost like males and females are a different species" (Leach 2009).

Further, Prof Graves predicted that the male Y chromosome, determinant of the male sex, was "on the path to extinction and could run out within the next five million years" — provided, of course, humans survive till then.

The recent revelation from chromosomal and genetic studies are truly challenging and throws light on the psychological behaviour of the two sexes.

Contemporary psychology reminds us that the basic human emotion of fear comes from our own powerlessness. Fear in the hands of authoritarian figures tends to become anger, while in the hands of submissive people, it tends to take the shape of sadness.

The general assumption is that the "physically strong but spiritually weak" males have been using power as a means not only for subjugation, but also for violence on themselves and on the environment.

Whereas women, who are considered "physically weak and spiritually deep," are prone to sadness together with their derivative emotions such as guilt, loneliness, depression, dejection and hurt.

In other words, negatively perceived, men tend to be aggressive and assertive, while women tend to be depressive and destructive. Aggression and destruction do not benefit either men or women. Such has been the game that genders have been playing for so long.

Confronted with the gigantic problems facing humanity today, we need to radically change the rules of game.

When we acknowledge and accept our basic human limitation — including the intrinsic spiritual emptiness — the need to play one against the other vanishes. Then we can open ourselves to wholeness — intellectual, psychological and spiritual — that we are capable of experiencing, differently and uniquely. Perceived thus, the normal fear that we experience can become a positive force that will enhance our survival value. Once we can accept our emptiness and are open to wholeness, the game of needless aggression and hopeless destruction will vanish.

So we do not have stronger or weaker sexes, but different sexes. We can then share power — collectively and individually — to transform ourselves. Once this happens, crucial social threats such as poverty, terrorist violence, environmental destruction and nuclear threat become our collective concerns, demanding immediate attention. The issues of gender differences and superiority/inferiority, though significant, can be seen from a different perspective — a liberative and holistic one.

26

Looking at Our Risks Objectively

We are wired to protect ourselves and to promote the life of others. But today, as reported in The New York Times, evidence is mounting that the brain systematically misjudges certain kinds of risks. In effect, evolution has programmed us to be alert for snakes and enemies with clubs, but we are not well prepared to respond to dangers that require forethought and considered reflection.

If we come across a cobra, nearly all of our brain will light up with activity as we react to the perceived "threat." Yet, if we hear about the nuclear bomb or radio-active poisoning that can destroy us totally, only a small part of the brain that focuses on the future — a portion of the prefrontal cortex in the brain — will light up.

"We humans do strange things, perhaps, because vestiges of our ancient brain still guide us in the modern world," claims Paul Slovic, a psychology professor (Kristof 2009). Let us consider two great challenges that humanity faces: One, malnutrition and abject poverty of millions of people who cannot sustain themselves. Though we are all aware of it, since it is not an "enemy with club" we tend to procrastinate to find a solution. Two, the climate warms, ice sheets melt and seas rise. People talk about it and we resolve to do a lot. But when it comes to action, we dilly-dally and ignore it.

On the other side, if the danger is of an immediate and visceral nature — such as the terror attacks in our neighbourhood — we will respond instantly and will become passionate about it.

"The threats that were dominant in our evolutionary history," observes Daniel Gilbert, a professor of psychology at Harvard University, demand our immediate attention. In contrast, he notes in The New York Times, the kinds of dangers that are most serious today — such as nuclear war, climate change or mass hunger — are swept aside by the brain (Kristof 2009).

At the University of Virginia, Professor Jonathan Haidt shows his Psychology students how evolution has prepared us to fear some things: He asks his students how many would be afraid to stand within 10 feet of a friend carrying a pet boa constrictor. Many hands go up, although almost none had been bitten by a snake. "The objects of our phobias, and the things that are actually dangerous to us, are almost unrelated in the modern world, but they were related in our ancient environment," Haidt said. So we are not programmed to fear gradually emerging crises or dangers (Kristof 2009).

For example, Americans spend nearly $700 billion a year on the military and less than a paltry $3 billion on the food and drugs administration, even though food poisoning kills more Americans than foreign armies and terrorists.

Still, according to these authors, all is not lost, particularly if we understand and acknowledge our neurological shortcomings properly and try to compensate adequately with rational analysis. If we humans really want, we have the foresight and the ability to provide intelligent solutions to save the planet and foster life.

Religious vision has a significant role in motivating us to move from our short-term goals to life-sustaining ones. It can help us to appreciate long-term risks. Religious wisdom can enable us to look at our personal and collective risks more objectively, offering more rational and collective analysis and solutions for the common good of humanity.

27

Children: Do the Parents Own Them?

Recently the Bombay High Court denied Niketa Mehta the permission to abort her 25-week-old foetus. Niketa and her husband Haresh had sought the court's approval since the child might be born with "congenital heart condition." Later, however, she had a miscarriage (Ghose 2008).

The verdict caught the nation's imagination instantly. Surfers poured their views on the internet, arguing for and against who should have the final say while deciding an abortion. In a limited poll conducted by an English news channel, 71.8 per cent of the netizens felt that parents should be the sole decision makers with regard to aborting a foetus.

The fierce battle between pro-choice and pro-life may be absent in India, unlike the West. So in this column, I am not going to speak against abortion, but will reflect on the role and value of life, even when it is fragile (Ghose 2008).

> "We are their only hope for their present and their future"

Of course, it is the right of every parent not only to take care of the child, but also to expect the best for the child. Since Indian society is, by and large, open to children, it is useful to raise the question: Whom does a child belong to?

In the first place, the child definitely belongs to the parents. But the limit does not end there. To proceed further, the child, in a different way, belongs to the larger family, to the village and then to the nation.

Taking the movement still further, the child truly belongs to the larger family of life or to the totality that is God.

So the responsibility of providing a suitable environment to children is not only limited to parents, but to the larger family and also to God. In the same way, taking the life of a child, even when it has not seen the light of the day, cannot be an exclusive privilege of the parents alone.

The larger society has to play a positive role in protecting children and fostering their precious and vulnerable life.

In this context, it is terrible to think of female infanticide that is prevalent in some parts of India. Abject poverty and forced labour in inhuman conditions that our children are subject to is also a serious concern to the larger Indian nation. No society, especially one that is rooted in its spiritual depth, can tolerate this.

Raising the standard of life of our children and providing them the basic necessities of life is our duty, both as Indians and as religious people.

Thus American motivational speaker Zig Ziglar is right when he said: "Our children are our only hope for the future, but we are their only hope for their present and their future" (Ziglar 2002).

The insights of the mystic-poet Khalil Gibran are valid even today (Gibran 1937):

Your children are not your children.
They are the sons and daughters of Life's longing for itself.
They come through you but not from you,
And though they are with you yet they belong not to you.

Truly, we need to learn to let life live through us.

28

Last Moments: Lead Us Back to Life?

On September 18, 2007, a computer science professor, Randy Pausch, stepped in front of an audience of 400 people at Carnegie Mellon University to deliver his last lecture called "Really achieving your childhood dreams" (Pausch and Zaslow 2008). It has become a hit in the internet world.

With slides of his CT scans beaming out to the audience, Randy told his audience about the cancer that was devouring his pancreas and that would claim his life in a matter of months. On the stage that day, Randy was youthful, energetic, handsome, often cheerfully and darkly funny. He seemed invincible. But this was a brief moment, as he himself acknowledged.

Randy's lecture has become a phenomenon in YouTube, as has the book he wrote based on the same principles. He urges the listeners "to live attentively" and "to celebrate the dreams we all strive to make realities." Sadly, Randy lost his battle to pancreatic cancer on July 25, 2008, but his legacy will continue to inspire us all, for generations to come.

In his talk and book, he is silent on religion and God.

Another popular writer, Sir Arthur Charles Clarke was a British science fiction author, inventor, and futurist, most famous for the movie, "2001: A Space Odyssey." The host and commentator in the British television series, "Mysterious World," was working on the last manuscript, aptly called, The Last Theorem, when he died in Sri Lanka on March 19, 2008.

What is interesting is that both the authors talk about the last things from an agnostic perspective. They urge us to take life seriously and live it authentically. Confronted with our last moments, so many things that we strive for, become relative and even useless.

In a way, all religions do contribute something significant to our understanding of death. Eschatology is the reflection on the last things and the final destiny of human beings. Bhagavan Rajneesh goes to the extent of asserting that "without death, there would not be religion."

Whether we are religious or not, confronting death leads us to appreciate life. Realising the last moment relativises so many of our present activities. Respectfully observing the death of a beloved one, helps us to appreciate him or her deeply.

Unfortunately, ours is a "death-denying" and "death-delaying" culture. We refuse to look straight into the eyes of death. Deep down, we are mortally afraid of death. We are terrified of it. Thus, our life, unfortunately, becomes nothing more than running away from itself. In the process, we do not enjoy anything, we do not even live our lives.

Death, "the possibility of the impossibility of our being" is an intrinsic part of our lives. Without encountering it, we cannot genuinely live. That is the spiritual wisdom of all religions, and even true humanism.

It is sad to see that so many of us "live our lives as if we won't die and die as if we have never lived!"

> "Idols must die so that symbols might live."
> Ricoeur

In this context, the remark of the Father of the Nation is insightful and inspiring: "Fear of death makes us devoid both of valour and religion. For, want of valour is want of religious faith." Authentic living and dying implies that we look at death and befriend it.

29

Respect the Body and Seek the Soul

Who am I? Have you ever wondered how to relate to your body and soul? Can one say: "I have a body!" or "I am my body!" The difference between these two is crucial to how we understand ourselves and the world.

Some of us like to regard our bodies as external to ourselves. Some would consider that it is not the body, but the soul that matters. The body is like a shirt that can be taken off and thrown away. Some very spiritual persons do tend to deny the body, disregard the senses and disparage the material world.

Some others, mainly materialists, like to consider that they are their bodies. They assure us that there is nothing "beyond" the body. According to them, all the chemical, emotional and spiritual activities of a human being stem from the body and are finally reducible to bodily functions. They glorify the body and assert that the soul is merely an epiphenomenon and is, hence, ephemeral.

Richard Dawkins, the famous atheist socio-biologist, claimed recently that in the next 50 years, science will be able to prove that the "soul" does not exist. Paul Ricoeur, a contemporary French philosopher, has taken a middle path and related the body and soul in a different way. He used the term "symbol" in a philosophical way and has shown that we can best describe the "body" as the "symbol" of the "soul." By this term, he means two very important characteristics of the body-soul relation (Ricoeur 1967).

First, we need the body to relate to the soul. Without the body, the soul is not accessible to us. So, the body is indispensable. Second, the soul is definitely larger than the body. So, the "soul" stands for the "depth-dimension" or the "surplus of meaning" that the body, to some extent, conveys to us.

He considers that the opposite of symbol is idol (Pandikattu 1996). An idol, according to Ricoeur, is something that does not "participate in" and "points to" something deeper. If a human being is reduced merely to the bodily dimension, it is a process of idolising.

Similarly, if a human being is considered exclusively as a "spiritual entity," without any bodily dimension, that is also a process of idolisation. The person wishes to regain the existential tension in the body-soul relationship. The soul is larger than the body. But the soul cannot be accessed by humans apart the body. Hence, the body, just like the soul, is indispensable.

Humans tend to choose the easy way out, by either reducing themselves to a body (reduction) or glorifying the person beyond the body as the soul (idealism). "Idols must die so that symbols might live." Only when we maintain this healthy tension, can we genuinely be spiritual in the contemporary world.

Taking the different dimensions of our existence seriously, many contemporary religious thinkers believe that we need a spirituality that respects the human body and elevates the material world. Without reducing the spirituality to the material, they plead that we respect the material and go beyond it.

So, I am body-soul, the body "pointing to" and "participating in" the soul (Marcel 2001).

30

Human Body Reveals the Truth

It is truly incredible to experience the dynamism, flexibility and versatility of the human body that most of us take for granted. Though earlier considered as something dirty and "below human dignity," today we realise more and more the uniqueness and greatness of the human body that is precious and precarious.

Recent scientific investigation, especially the neuro-linguistic programme (NLP) that has become popular in the past few decades, talks of the basic sensitivity inherent in the body. For instance, left to itself, body reacts creatively to external stimuli and always reveals the truth. "The human body just does not lie," claims Dr Dick McHugh, the well-known NLP expert who brought it to India. He explains that, though we often lie, it is because of our mind. Our mind is capable of deceiving others and ourselves. Due to the inherent cravings and dislikes that we have, the mind is capable of twisting facts, pretending and even creating its own illusory world. But human body, freed from the control of the mind, always reveals the truth.

For instance, recent studies have revealed that human body reacts faster than even feelings and words. So paying close attention to the body can reveal the truth of oneself, even before a word is uttered. One of the easiest ways that the body reveals itself is through breath. The way one breathes indicates the way one feels. Even before uttering a word, paying attention to one's breath - whether it is regular, deep, erratic or fast - tells a lot about one's emotional state.

Definitely, the mind can control the body consciously and fake bodily responses. But even before the mind exercises control over the body, a sensitive person can detect the genuine feelings by observing the body sensations intensely.

Since the body naturally does not lie, it takes tremendous amount of work to make the body fit into an artificial response. In fact, it is much easier to let the body relax and then listen to the body. By doing so, we shall be opening ourselves to the powerful unconscious at work in us, which enables one to tap the strength and resource from within.

It is true that so much of resource – be it for healing or even for spiritual strength – is latently present in our body. It does not even require much work to have recourse to this power. What is required is to remove from the body the tension and stiffness that we have artificially created through our mental concoctions.

So, the easiest way for one to live a healthy life and be spiritually attentive is to draw from the inner resource of our own body. Respecting the body, taking care of it and acknowledging the preciousness of our own bodies is the first step. Then letting the body relax – using yoga or awareness exercises – can work wonders.

So, the dated notion that body is a "prison house" and has to be enslaved to be a liberated person is wrong. In fact, techniques like vipassana or tantric meditations show that body is the "temple of God" where we can be totally at home. When we are totally at home with our own fragile and precious body – with all its strengths and vulnerabilities – and own it up, we are on road to liberation and wholeness of life. Then we shall be open to the truth of ourselves – that our body does not lie and that we can be open to the truth of our own body and so be liberated.

31

Nicolaus Copernicus: Revolution Beyond "I"

Nicolaus Copernicus was the first astronomer to formulate a scientifically-based theory that displaced the Earth from the centre of the universe. His epochal book, *De revolutionibus orbium coelestium* (On the Revolutions of the Celestial Spheres), is often regarded as the starting point of modern astronomy (Copernicus 1966).

Although Greek, Indian and Muslim savants had published heliocentric hypotheses centuries before Copernicus, his publication of a scientific theory of heliocentrism, demonstrating that the motions of celestial objects can be explained without putting the Earth at the centre of the universe, became a landmark in the history of modern science, that is known as the Copernican Revolution. Recently the resting place and remains of the 16th century astronomer-priest Nicolaus Copernicus have been positively identified, researchers in Poland announced.

The discovery, according to reports, was made by comparing DNA from a skeleton found in 2005 and his hair found in Sweden. Polish archaeologist Jerzy Gassowski said that forensic facial reconstruction of the skull bears a striking resemblance to existing portraits of Copernicus (Bowcott 2008).

The finding ends centuries-long speculation on the astronomer's final resting place. It may be mentioned that his skull was found buried in a Roman Catholic Cathedral in Poland. The most vital aspect of Copernicus' work is that it forever changed the place of humans in the cosmos; no longer could we legitimately regard our significance to be greater than our fellow creatures. With Copernicus' work, humans took their place along with and not against other creatures.

So the great German poet and philosopher Goethe affirms: "Of all discoveries and opinions, none may have exerted a greater effect on the human spirit than the doctrine of Copernicus. The world had scarcely become known as round and complete in itself when it was asked to waive the tremendous privilege of being the centre of the universe. Never, perhaps, was a greater demand made on humankind - for by this admission so many things vanished in mist and smoke! What became of our Eden, our world of innocence, piety and poetry; the testimony of the senses; the conviction of a poetic — religious faith? No wonder his contemporaries did not wish to let all this go and offered every possible resistance to a doctrine which in its contents authorised and demanded a freedom of view and greatness of thought so far unknown, indeed not even dreamed of."

We do acknowledge that our present generation has gained a lot from his scientific insights. But have we really made our own the psychological and religious insight from the Copernican revolution: that I am not the centre of the universe? That my ego is not the absolute? That my life is not the most important thing in the world? That my view may not be the greatest? That my in-group need not be the best and greatest? A genuine person realises that her uniqueness comes not by being better than the other. She has her own intrinsic worth. Such a Copernican revolution at the psychological and spiritual realm will make us both sober and realistic. That could be a self-emptying affirmation and could liberate us from our narrowness, bigotry and prejudices. That would enable us to rejoice truly in the happiness of others for their own sake.

32

Resurrection of the Body

Christians throughout the world celebrate the resurrection of Jesus, which is their most significant celebration. It is, in fact, this "foundational" experience of Christians that gave birth to their faith and tradition.

One of the really special features of this faith is the belief among Christians of their own individual bodily resurrection. In other words, Christians believe that there is life after death and that such a "life after life" is best characterised by body.

> The self is the centre of the "narrative identity" which constitutes me.

Such a belief is suspicious to some Christians themselves. Many good believers can easily think of the immortality of the soul and the possible life after the death of the soul. It has almost become scandalous to believe in the possibility of survival and even glorified resurrection of the body.

What does resurrection of the body mean to us today? First, it is quite different from the immortality of the soul. In fact, popularly understood souls do not die and so it is superfluous to speak of the resurrection of the soul.

Second, resurrection of the body takes our individual death seriously. Unlike the heroic death of Socrates or Vinoba Bhave, Jesus did not die a stoic death. He suffered and underwent the humiliating and tragic experience of death. So, for Christians, death with all its abomination is a despicable act.

Third, resurrection of the body implies that we take the body and this world earnestly. This world is not maya, the body is not an illusion. We do not live in samsara. Everything that happens to the body and to one's own history is significant and meaningful. So, the commitment to the world and our efforts to improve the condition of the world are of utmost importance. Thus the resurrection in the body implies that we take the worldly concerns as integral part of the spiritual sadhana or exercise. Fourth, resurrection of the body does not imply revival of the same physical body. It is not resuscitation, where humans rise with the same physical body, with the same physical features and characteristics. Such a revival is impossible because of the simple physical fact that my body disintegrates and, in fact, becomes part of the body of another person in the course of history.

Finally, what is really my body? It is definitely physical, but it is not a crass material thing. In fact, my body, which is primarily material, also enables relationship or interaction with the world and with others. My body enables me to experience the deeper self or soul that I am. So the body is the totality of relationship or contacts that I establish with myself, with others and with God.

Understood thus, the body is the "reflection" or "symbol" of the self. The self is the centre of the "narrative identity" which constitutes me. It is the basis or foundation of the enabling and unfolding possibilities of myself.

As such, the body is a great mystery. It is definitely not the soul, but very closely related to it and leads to it. The body is not mere matter but born of it. The body is the limited self in search of the larger me. Interestingly, the other great Christian feast, Christmas, also refers to this insight. Christmas is the great mystery where God takes on "flesh and blood" and "dwells among us." So, there is no way Christianity can get away from its basic assertion of the bodily nature of life after death. That is the insight we can gain from the Christian belief in the resurrection of the body.

Reality and Paradox

33

The Reality: Its Seven Colours

As children, we marvel at the colours of the rainbow. As adults, we are fascinated by the colours of nature. It is generally accepted that light is composed of seven colours, which can be shown through experiments using a prism.

We make a distinction between "primary" and "secondary" colours. The first thing to realise is that the number of "primary" colours depends on the type of creature that is doing the looking. Normal cones in the human eye sense light in broad colour bands in the red, green and blue-violet regions of the spectrum. Thus, for humans, mixing various amounts of three colours of light (red, green and blue) will produce all colours that can be perceived. That is true for an additive source such as a computer monitor or a television screen that produces light.

The eye is sensitive to broad bands of light wavelengths, and thus it interpolates colours depending which of the three cones are receiving light. Colour is actually how our eyes and brain interpret light. Our eyes can only see radiation with a wavelength of 380 nanometres to 740 nanometres. Further, there are two ways to make "yellow" light. First, we can use equal amounts of red and green light. These stimulate the red and green cones, and the brain sees "yellow." Second, we can use a wavelength of light that is between red and green (about 565nm). Because the response of the red and green cones overlaps, this colour also stimulates both the red and green cones. The brain sees "yellow" in both cases.

For pictures using paint or ink, it gets a little complicated because what happens to the light before it strikes the eye is a two-step process. Inks are subtractive. They block various colours of light and only the colours that are not blocked are reflected from the paper to your eyes.

In fact, there is rarely light of a pure colour. Instead, an object appears red because it absorbs all colours except red. The red light is reflected on our eyes. This difference is why you perceive white light when you mix red, green, and blue light sources, but if you mix red, green and blue, you get black. Red colour absorbs green and blue, green absorbs red and blue and blue absorbs red and green. The net result is all colours get absorbed and you perceive black. There are three types of colour blindness, depending on which colour sensor is defective.

How many colours can the eye distinguish? The published literature is remarkably inefficient at providing an answer to this important question. According to an oft-quoted reference, 10 million surface colours can be distinguished by the normal human eye under optimum observing conditions. Other estimates put it at just one lakh colours.[9]

Dogs seem to have only two kinds of colour receptors. They see fewer separate colours. Many birds have four or more types of cones (the extra one is ultraviolet). They see potentially many more colours than humans, depending on how the brain perceives this colour. Birds would use a television with four primary colours. These questions raise some larger philosophical and religious issues: Does colour really exist? Does it exist apart from humans who perceive them? What justification do we have to classify colours? How many colours, in fact, exist? Isn't our recourse to reality enabled and limited by our colour perception? Will dogs and birds have a different perception of colour and reality? Isn't material reality much more complex than that perceived by our eyes?

34

The Brain: Its Five Senses

The five senses work together all the time to allow our body to function properly in the world. The brain, in fact, is the centre of the sensual body.

> Reality is far grander and greater than our wonderful senses can perceive.

To see something, light bounces off the object we are looking at into the pupil. This light crosses the lens and the images get focused upside down. The object shines on the retina of the eye. Then, the optic nerve carries the picture we see and the message goes to the brain. What the brain does after the message goes to it is that it turns the picture the right side up. Then it figures out what we are seeing and how we should respond to it. Having two eyes increases our angle of vision and helps us to judge depth. Two eyes also allow us to see 180 degrees and three-dimensional objects.

Our ears send information about sounds to the brain in the form of nerve impulses. Sounds are collected in the outer ear and are sent through the ear canal to the eardrum. Three small bones in the middle part of the ear make sounds louder. The receptor cells send impulses to the auditory nerve, which goes to the brain. The brain receives impulses from the auditory nerve and gives meaning to the sound impulses. We have two ears because sound hits one ear a fraction of a second before the other and produces stronger vibrations. This helps us to sense the direction of the sound.

Taste helps us to determine the flavour and palatability of food. It even signals dangerous gases and toxic food. All over our tongue, there are little bumps called taste buds. There are four different types of taste buds, sweet, sour, bitter or salty things.

Touch enables our skin to have physical contact with another object. Touch or sensory receptors are located in clusters around the skin. When these are squeezed, the layers rub against each other causing an electrical nerve impulse. The most sensitive touch receptors are located at the face, back of the neck and chest.

Skin works together with the hypothalamus, which contains heat and cold-sensitive cells. The hypothalamus responds by increasing the number of nerve impulses transmitted by the brain. Skin helps to regulate temperature preventing excess heat (hyperthermia) or dearth of it (hypothermia).

Every time we breathe, air flows through the nasal cavity, facilitating the flow down through the back of the mouth into the throat. Simultaneously, some of it passes to the olfactory organs. Any odour molecules in the air pass by and get stuck to the mucous in the nose. The hair senses the odour and transmits messages to the brain. Your brain, therefore, knows the odour. The smell receptor cell is located high up behind the nose.

These five senses are our window on the world. All our technologies are extensions of our senses. Senses are more intimately connected with our brain than we think. So, the larger questions connected with the senses are: Are there other senses that we are unaware of? Is the mind another sense, as implied by Indian philosophy? If humans had collectively lacked one sense or had one more of it, how would our world look like? In fact, we are enabled and imprisoned by our five senses. We are captivated by and captured by our senses. Reality is far grander and greater than our wonderful senses can perceive.

35

The Existence: Its Three Dimensions

We are fortunate enough to live in a three-dimensional world. The length, breadth and height constitute the space around us and the reality that is us. It is marvellous to experience the depth that is possible only in a three-dimensional world.

It is possible for us to image dimensions less than three. In the simplified one-dimensional world, an ant — that has only length — can walk back and forth on a string that is stretched tight. Unaware of the other dimensions around it, the ant lives in a happy but isolated world. The being on a two-dimensional world can walk on the surface of a perfectly plain glass, enjoy seeing the whole 360 degrees around it. But if a human being puts a coin on the glass, the appearance of the coin will be a miracle for this being. The downpour will be another unexplained miracle for this being. Even basic features such as absorption or digestion of food will be impossible for such a poor two-dimensional creature. The three-dimensional world around us enables us to experience the fabulous reality as we see it. But the mathematics of dimensions does not put any limit to it. Strictly speaking, we can have more than three dimensions, which will be impossible for us to imagine.

Some versions of the super string theory in physics assumes that reality has 11 dimensions (M-theory). They assume right at the beginning of the universe that all these dimensions were active. Later, they folded themselves up and so at present we can perceive only three dimensions. "Imagining the Tenth Dimension" by Rob

Bryanton is an insightful and controversial book (Bryanton 2006). The philosophical and religious challenges posed by these speculations are tremendous. When religions try to approach the ultimate reality, are we talking of more dimensional existence? What would life after death look like? Is it a continuation of our space-time existence or a dimensionally different mode of existence?

God, the object of all religions, must be experienced by us in our three dimensional world. But that does not imply that God is limited to the three dimensions only. If he is the Lord of creation, he would have created the other dimensions too. But it is possible that he would exist in a radically new dimension with the possibility of intervening in our three-dimensional world. Just as a two-dimensional being cannot understand how a coin has appeared on the surface of the glass, maybe we are limited beings, who cannot experience the full depth and complexity of the rich physical reality around us?

> We need to go beyond a merely individualistic morality.

Further, if human beings are able to create initial conditions similar to Big Bang, as it is being tried at CERN, Switzerland, do we reach closer to the complexity of reality? Will it be possible for humans to add new dimensions to their existence? My answer is: These questions are profound and worth pursuing. They do add to the magnificent data available to humanity that we can truly marvel at. They do challenge the way we live our spiritual and religious life. So the possibility of new discoveries by physicists must excite us. At the same time, we must remember that we have not exhausted the mystery and complexity of the three-dimensional world of which we are sure. Let us truly continue to marvel at the robustness and roughness of the three-dimensional being of ours! But we can and must remain open to further realms of possibilities. The reality is truly and marvellously complex.

36

The Time: Its One Direction

It is truism to say that we live in time. Time enables us to be born, to grow, to mature and finally to blow out. Time with its past, present and future is a key enigma. We are not much better than St Augustine who claimed 1,500 years ago: "I do know what time is if you do not ask me; but if you ask me I do not know."

A simplistic view of the three aspects of time helps us to cope with the normal routine of life. But let us remember that the past is not merely something that happened previously. Events in the past shape our present and memory of the past helps us to live the present. Philosophers are of the opinion that the "remembrance of the things of the past" truly makes the present. In the same way, the future is not just something that will happen. We anticipate the future just now. Without that hope and anticipation of the future, the present does not make sense.

So, the usual linear description of time as being divided into past, present and future is simplistic and inadequate, though useful. We need to appreciate the complex dimensions of the past intermingling with the present and being carried over into the future. The present now that we experience is, in fact, constituted also by the memory of the past and anticipation of the future.

> "This too will pass away?"

One crucial difference of time, compared with other dimensions of reality, is its direction? Why does time always flow forward? In the case of space, we know we can move forward or backward and no restrictions are placed. At the mathematical level, too, we have time moving back and forth. What makes human life possible, as we know it, is this unique directionality of time.

The theory of relativity does take this directionality of time seriously. Most of us have not accepted the significance of the simple conclusion of the theory of relativity: that time is relative to the frame of reference. In other words, the "common-sense" notion of time is possible only under certain limited conditions.

Time, thus, provides us with one of the enduring mysteries of reality and life. Many of our common-sense notions of everyday life are shattered by scientific discoveries.

Further, according to the theory of relativity, under certain conditions, the simultaneity of two events cannot be always assumed. So too in some rare cases involving quantum particles, the distinction between the past and the future vanishes. This has spurred the imagination of science-fiction writers, who enable one to travel back in time. What would happen if I were to go back in time and eliminate my grandmother? Can I prevent my own birth, then?

Such questions have a deeper significance. If we live in a four (or even 11) dimensional space, what really limits or enables the directionality of time? What enables time to move only in one direction? Why can't it at least move sideways?

Physicists answer these questions by bringing in the law of entropy. Though physics can legitimately seek such answers, the metaphysical and religious quests cannot be ignored. In fact, the metaphysical questions on time help us to marvel truly at the very nature of this life-sustaining reality.

But the more profound query: Why is reality so construed that beings like us can grow, mature and die? What enables us to experience the joys and sadness of life and affirm, "This too will pass away?"

37

The World: Rough and Tough

Everyone knows that we live in a four-dimensional world. Albert Einstein's imagination and ingenuity have enabled us to change our way of visualising the world.

Our four-dimensional world consists of three dimensions of space and one of time. We can make sense of our life experiences because of the dimensionality of our existence.

According to the three-dimensional understanding, we have a point with zero dimension, since a point is supposed to have no length, breadth or height. Then we have a line with one dimension, a plane or circle with two and a cube with three dimensions.

But the only trouble is that, though we know them so well, none can ever experience a zero-dimensional point or a one-dimensional line. It is due to the ingenuity and creativity of our imagination that we live in the three dimensions of space. That is the ideal world that we can so proudly imagine.

Real objects in space (do objects still "exist" in space, even after Einstein's relativity theories?) are never three-dimensional. In the real world, we don't have any circles, but we have figures that approximate a circle. We do not have any cubes, but objects that approach three dimensions.

A few years ago, the Polish mathematician Benoit Mendelbrot had introduced the notion of fractals to describe such objects in the real world. Fractals are objects with fractional dimension. Using complex numbers and advanced mathematics, he showed the world that real objects, such as a stone, could have a fractional dimension like 2.17676.

Though we cannot easily follow the mathematics behind it, fractals indicate the roughness and self-similarity present in a real material object. Fractals indicate how "rough" or "curved" a surface is in the real world.

The popularity of fractals is due to the extremely fascinating colours and contours that they are able to produce in the computer world.

Fractals tell us about the relationship between the ideal and the real world. Using our mental categories, we have been able to successfully project or idealise the world. We have also been successful in reapplying this idealisation back to the real world. But it doesn't prevent us from acknowledging the "rough" nature of the real world.

In fact, a little reflection will convince us that we live in a tensional relationship between the "real" and the "ideal." Every word we use, not merely abstract nouns, is, in fact, an "idea" based on the real world. A simple word such as "mother" is a generalisation and abstraction based on the experience of real mothers.

"God" is the best projection or idealisation that we have. As Sigmund Freud reminds us, he is the projection of our ideals. That doesn't imply that God doesn't exist. It implies that our mind operates through the process of idealisation, generalisation and application to the concrete.

The real world — which is the immediate source of our experiences and even that of God — is not perfect. It is rough, uneven and most of the time idiosyncratic. That is our precious world, from which we draw the noblest ideals and insights.

So, the roughness of the real world should help us to keep our feet on earth and at the same time lift our spirit to the highest! The paradox of the real versus the ideal is something that we experience not just in our spiritual world, but in our world of daily life.

38

Happiness: Ever Approachable, Never Attainable

Though the Big Bang theory has not found acceptance with all scientists, it is still the most popular theory we have regarding the origin of the universe. Cosmological models of the "Big Bang" expansion of the universe have converged on a general framework in time, energy and temperature. Below is an attempt to show some of the features of the models on a timeline, as explained in the bestseller, "The First Three Minutes," by Nobel Laureate Stephen Weinberg (Weinberg 1993).

> God: ever approachable and never attainable.

An overwhelming weight of evidence has convinced cosmologists that the universe came into existence at a definite moment in time, some 13 billion years ago, in the form of a super hot, super dense fireball of energetic radiation. Until the arrival of this Big Bang theory, the universe was believed to be essentially eternal and unchanging, represented by the steady state model.

The Big Bang did not begin as a huge explosion within the universe, the Big Bang created the universe. A popular misconception is that it happened within the universe. This causes people to wonder as to where in the universe it started, as if by running the clock backwards we would reach the point where all the galaxies come together in the centre of the universe. The universe doesn't have a centre just as the surface of a sphere doesn't have a centre. The standard model of the Big Bang theory proposes that the universe emerged from a singularity, at time zero, and describes all that has happened since 0.0001 of a second after this moment of creation. The temperature at that time was 1,000 billion degrees Kelvin and the universe had the same density as the nuclear matter, 1014 gram per cubic centimetre.

Under these extreme conditions, the photons of the 'background' radiation carry so much energy that they are interchangeable with particles. Photons create pairs of particles and anti-particles, which annihilate one another to make energetic photons in a constant interchange of energy. Because of a small asymmetry in the way the fundamental interactions work, slightly more particles were produced than anti-particles — about one in a billion more particles than anti-particles. When the universe had cooled to the point that photons no longer had the energy required to make particles, all the paired particles and anti-particles annihilated, and the one in a billion particles left over became stable matter.

One-hundredth of a second after time zero, the temperature had fallen 90 per cent to 100 billion K. By one-tenth of a second after time zero, the temperature was down to 30 billion K. After 13.8 seconds, it was down to 3 billion K, and by three minutes and two seconds it had cooled to 1 billion K, only 70 times hotter than the centre of the sun today. At this temperature, nuclei of deuterium and helium could be formed and stick together despite collisions with other particles.

What is insightful is that astrophysicists have been able to describe the phenomenon of the Big Bang up to three minutes with a very high degree of precision. They can trace its origin to, say, 0.0001 seconds after its beginning. To investigate it more becomes quite difficult, and finally almost impossible. To describe the phenomenon closest to zero, you need to spend almost an infinite amount of energy. So it is ever approachable and never attainable. So many things in human life are also so: our ideals, perfection and even happiness (Pandikattu 2009).

39

Human Life: Finite Search for Infinite

Human beings are open to the infinite and, at the same time, bound to the concrete. At every moment of our lives, we experience this tension between the finite and the infinite.

Taking the case of feeling, or affection, these two directions are evident in terms of: pleasure and happiness. The finite pole is to be found in pleasure, which is immediately met and terminates in finite acts. Pleasure is the movement of feeling towards the good fulfilled in the instant. As such, it is precarious and perishable. The finite pole's focus is on its bond with bodily life and the fulfilment of bodily needs and desires. Pleasure stands at the level of condition for all other good. In itself, pleasure has its own type of totality and is non-reducible. It has an "innocence," but it is a "menaced innocence" in that the potential for conflict is present with that of happiness. The pole of infinitude in the feeling is happiness, bliss or *ananda*. Happiness or blissfulness is that dimension of feeling that revolves around the need for unity or wholeness in human life. It terminates in the existential project, which is our infinite destiny. The feeling of happiness is intimately connected to the idea of well-being. But it is more than a mere idea, since it is the fulfilment of this direction in absolute bliss (Pandikattu 1999).

So we can perceive human affectivity and its two dynamic polarities of finitude and infinite. The infinite in us is both bound and enabled by the finite. We remain always open to the infinite and rooted to the finite. The swing makes us the unique creature that we are. It is in this unique "in-betweenness" that we can situate and understand our own freedom (Pandikattu 2000).

In fact, human being is an infinite God who is bound to the finite matter; as a finite being who reaches out to the unlimited, we lead a "tensional existence." There emerges the precious freedom that we are capable of. There we also perceive our fragility. It is precisely in its fragility that the beauty and uniqueness of human beings shines forth! So author Albert Camus could exclaim, "Man is the only creature that refuses to be what he is" (Camus 1991).

Given such a human situation, where the voluntary is in the involuntary, the material is in the spiritual, the quest for human nature and freedom will always remain precarious. The urge to reach out to the infinite will enable us to remain humans. This quest can be stifled only at the cost our humanness. Thus, humans are limited, embraced by the unlimited, with the material overwhelmed by the spiritual.

Just as a material reality is ever approachable, but never attainable, human beings also can be understood in this paradoxical and ambiguous manner. So it is ever approachable and never attainable. So human beings, including our ideals, perfections, our friendship and even happiness, are approachable but never completely realisable.

Precisely therein lies the precious and precarious nature of human beings, their greatness and fragility. In such a scenario, it is our human endeavour to make sense of this ambiguous project that is human life. So, the role of philosophy is to mediate these two tensional aspects of life: that of the material and the beyond. If we understand this by religion — the spiritual realm, and by science — the material, then we can understand the insight of philosopher A. N. Whitehead that, "philosophy attains its chief importance by fusing ... religion and science into one rational scheme of thought" (Whitehead, Griffin et al. 1978).

40

Bernard d'Espagnat: Beyond Space, Time

The Templeton Prize "honours a living person who has made an exceptional contribution to affirming life's spiritual dimension, whether through insight, discovery, or practical works." The 2009 prize was presented to French physicist Bernard d'Espagnat.

In "The Guardian," d'Espagnat said: "I believe that some of our most engrained notions about space and causality should be reconsidered. Anyone who takes quantum mechanics seriously will have reached the same conclusion" (d'Espagnat 2009).

d'Espagnat's work was on experimental tests of Bell's theorem. This theorem states that either quantum mechanics is a complete description of the world or that if there is some reality beneath quantum mechanics, it must be non-local — that is, things can influence one another instantaneously, regardless of how much space stretches between them, violating Einstein's assertion that nothing can travel faster than the speed of light (d'Espagnat 2006).

But what d'Espagnat was really interested in was its significance for the nature of ultimate reality. From the mid-1960s, d'Espagnat was a philosophical visionary.

The BBC reported, "Prof. d'Espagnat's scientific pedigree puts him at the centre of the growth of quantum mechanics, working with Nobel laureates in the field, including Enrico Fermi and Niels Bohr. But he was troubled by how little the field was addressing the philosophical questions raised by the theory —which for the first time suggested that experiments were not measuring an absolute reality" (BBC_Correspondent 2009).

Speaking to the "Christian Science Monitor," d'Espagnat suggested that a key insight of quantum mechanics was to show that science does not provide a view of "ultimate reality as it really is" but rather "as it appears to us, accounting for the limitations of our own mind and our own sensibilities" (Templeton_Report_Correspondent 2009).

d'Espagnat opines that science has helped him to "justify his impression of a link between beauty and the divine." He said: "When we hear great classical music or look at very great paintings, they are not just illusions, but could be a revelation of something fundamental. I would accept calling it God or divine or godhead but with the restriction that it cannot be conceptualised for the very reason that this ultimate reality is beyond any concept that we can construct."

Unlike classical physics, quantum mechanics cannot describe the world as it really is, it can merely make predictions for the outcomes of our observations. If we want to believe, as Einstein did, that there is a reality independent of our observations, then this reality can either be knowable, unknowable or veiled. d'Espagnat subscribes to the third view. Through science, d'Espagnat says, we can glimpse some basic structures of the reality beneath the veil, but much of it remains an infinite, eternal mystery.

"There must exist, beyond mere appearances … a 'veiled reality' that science does not describe, but only glimpses uncertainty. In turn, contrary to those who claim that matter is the only reality, the possibility that other means, including spirituality, may also provide a window on ultimate reality cannot be ruled out, even by cogent scientific arguments" (Lehr 2009). d'Espagnat calls this veiled reality a being or independent reality or even "a great, hypercosmic God." It is a holistic, non-material realm that lies outside of space and time. Such an "independent reality plays, in a way, the role of God."

> "Peace cannot be kept by force; it can only be achieved by understanding."
> Einstein

Difference and Devotion

41

Our Martyrs' Deeds Must Not Go Waste

Henry Allinham, the world's oldest man, died on July 18, 2009 in London. He was 113 years old. He went to war as a teenager, helped keep flimsy aircraft flying, survived his wounds and came home from World War I to a long – very long — and fruitful life. Though he attributed his remarkable longevity to "cigarettes, whisky and wild, wild women," he was a modest man who served as Britain's conscience, reminding young people time and time again about the true cost of war (Associated_Press 2009).

"I want everyone to know," he told Associated Press during an interview in November, 2008. "They died for us." Allingham remained outspoken until his death, pleading for peace and begging anyone who would listen to remember those who died. "I think we need to make people aware that a few men gave all they had to give so that you could have a better world to live in," he said. "We have to pray it never happens again."

On July 26, 2009, Indians celebrated the 10th anniversary of the Kargil war and honoured the martyrs who sacrificed their lives in the war. Hundreds of soldiers who died and the many who were maimed deserve our genuine gratitude. At the same time, we must remember that the greatest tribute we can give to these privileged heroes is to live, so that they do not have to die again. In fact, we owe our existence to them: to generations in the past, who have offered everything so that we may grow up and experience peace.

The greatest disservice we can do to them is to sacrifice more people for the cause that they died for. Tragically, we do not seem to have learnt any lesson from their loss: lessons to promote collective peace and prosperity of our citizens.

It is not enough to erect monuments to remember the fallen heroes. It is not enough to pay homage to them on their anniversaries. In order to remember them gratefully, we need to actively protect life, promote peace and foster the well-being of all.

This cannot be achieved by technology alone. We need a sustained and collective effort, drawn from our rich religious and cultural heritage, to promote attitudes of peace in individuals so that we can establish a society that is at peace with itself and with each other. Only then do we honour the dead, so that more need not die for us to survive. But we do realise that good intentions alone are insufficient to create such a society where everyone can live with dignity. Individual efforts are very important, but insufficient. Collective work and conscious planning are needed, but are inadequate. After having worked for peace, we need to open ourselves to the infinite and pray for peace.

Albert Einstein reminds us that "Peace cannot be kept by force; it can only be achieved by understanding." To reach such an understanding and appreciation of each other, we need to free ourselves of egoism, envy and jealousy, individually and collectively. Lord Buddha is definitely right: "Those who are free of resentful thoughts surely find peace."

Though it is possible to rid ourselves of resentful thoughts at an individual level, it becomes much more difficult to do so at the collective or social level. Without honestly encountering ourselves — our weakness and sinfulness — we cannot get rid of our egoism and resentfulness.

We owe at least this to our past generation: To those who have made our living possible. They deserve not only our fond memories, but our committed, sustained action to promote peace and well-being.

42

Finest Homage to the Departed

The sudden and tragic death of YS Rajasekhara Reddy, the Chief Minister of Andhra Pradesh, India, on September 2, 2009, shocked many of us. What is still more frightening is the fact that hundreds of people are said to have taken their own lives on account of this great man's death. When we consider his death with those of others who committed suicide for his sake, we need to ask ourselves: How do we cope with death as such?

In a world where we "live as if we would never die and die as if we have never lived," the general temptation is to ignore death altogether. Still, it is to be noted that death can very well be a reaffirmation of life and can truly give us valuable insights into life. Confronted with death, be it of a beloved or a great hero, the three phases that we need to go through are: grieve, give and grow.

We need to take the death of our "significant ones" earnestly. We need to give ourselves the time and the space to realise that they are no more and we need to acknowledge the sadness that we truly feel. It is good to give enough time to experience the loss, the tragedy and so to grieve. Grieving the death of near ones is extremely crucial for the living. It has both therapeutic and cathartic effects.

After having felt the sadness intensely, it is time to enter into a dialogue with the departed. We need to talk to her and give to her many things we could not give her while she was alive. So many things we took for granted and never shared, we need to make up for all these at least at the moment of farewell.

Further, we need to give her a part of our lives, assure her that we will continue to be a part of her. It is the time to feel genuinely sorry for the unacknowledged harm that we might have done to her and to show our unexpressed and immense gratitude to her.

At this stage, we also need to acknowledge the loss of the beloved and learn to give her up. Though painful, the process of the funeral or cremation is a socially sanctioned help to make the giving up easy. The physical tragedy of death can be complete only when we give her up emotionally, and that may need more time.

The third step is to grow from the terrible experience of the death of a dear one. In a way, the living have a responsibility to the dead, to further their message. Also, the living need to learn from the dead to be more authentic. The growth that comes after proper grieving and giving up is an enabling one, which helps the departed to live in us and through us. Such a growth is possible only when we feel comfortable with a dialogue with the departed and to feel her warm presence in our lives.

If these steps of grieving for, giving up and growing out have not been adequately done, the tragedy of the death of a beloved will continue to afflict us. That would be a further tragedy, which paralyses the life of the living.

In the mysterious nature of life, we do know that death has a necessary role, which we do not fully fathom. But we do not know that without properly acknowledging and experiencing the death of those close to us, we do not allow ourselves to live. If we can adequately bid farewell to the departed, it would help us to make our present lives more meaningful. To live gratefully, gracefully and greatly is the finest homage we can pay to the departed.

43

A Little Dew that Makes Up the Ocean

Parables and stories have the power to reveal the deepest wisdom in life and the need for awareness to transform our lives. They speak directly to our heart. They are first lived — individually and collectively – and then told and retold.

I came across a recent book, "A Dewdrop in the Ocean: Wisdom Stories for Turbulent Time," by Francis J Padinjarekara. It contains life-transforming wisdom capsules for contemporary men and women (Padinjarekara 2009).

Here are some selected gems: "Suffering transforms human beings," commented the sage… "Ultimately it is not what happens to us but what happens in us that counts." "Judgements are most inefficient," the sage stated. "And a major waste of energy."… Intelligence involves appropriate response to situations — like calling attention to being unduly delayed or a decision to let something be… Or you can be judgemental, get angry, create distance or start a fight."

"Among the sage's friends and acquaintances were celebrities, business tycoons and other wealthy people. However, his life was very simple and none of the glitter has entered his home or life. When someone asked him why his lifestyle remained unaffected, a disciple spoke: "When a rose is set beside a diamond necklace, the rose doesn't shine, but the necklace may receive some of the perfume."

The insights offered are meditational, and even transformational. No book can save us unless we allow its insights to touch us. This book enables perceptive readers to have an "expansive sense of wonder" that one experiences when life's truths are disclosed. Each message is different from the other yet so beautifully linked because of its deep comprehension of the nature of life and reality.

Following the tradition of great spiritual masters such as Rajneesh or Anthony de Mello, the author attempts to spread transforming spiritual experiences in a non-invasive and welcoming manner. The wisdom in this book — like in a classic of any tradition — is subtle, yielding only to sustained inquiry. The relevance of topics and the utter simplicity with which profound truths are conveyed are masterly.

"The foundation and the basic test of any spirituality is not just how beautiful and uplifting it appears but how practical it is and how it enables us to live our lives and find our happiness in the world." In this sense, the author urges the practitioners to have both inner freedom and external commitment. Freed from the compulsions of ego, a healthy spirituality reaches out to others in joy and service. In such a process, the divine is encountered and awakening happens. Awakening just is. It is not the result of persistent planning and hard work.

Perceived thus, human life can very well be understood and appreciated as a "dew drop in the ocean." I am not the ocean. I do not have control over everything, including myself. Yet, in my never-ending quest for the unfolding truth, I am a puny little dew that makes up the ocean. I am aware of it and am part of it. Precisely therein lies my greatness.

Such an awareness opens me to see the ordinary things in my life in an extraordinary manner. Contemplation of such existence enables me "to see the world in a grain of sand and eternity in an hour," as poet William Blake has immortalised in his "Auguries of Innocence" (Blake, Sampson et al. 1975). Blake reminds us further: "A Robin Red breast in a Cage/ Puts all Heaven in a Rage/ A dog starv'd at his Master's Gate/ Predicts the ruin of the State" (Blake 1976).

44

Measuring Values

The Central Board of Secondary Education (CBSE), New Delhi, India, which is in the process of replacing marks with grades, may have stepped on something rather controversial and challenging. In addition to grades for academics and extra-curricular activities, students will now be graded on their attitude towards teachers, classmates, school programmes and the environment. They will also be graded on their value system, communication skills and interpersonal relationships.

> "The child is laughing: The Game is my wisdom, love and work/ The young is singing: The Love is my wisdom, work and game/ The adult is thinking: The Work is my wisdom, love and game./ The old is silent: The Wisdom is my love, game and work." Blaga

In a circular, CBSE said that classes IX and X will be going through continuous and comprehensive evaluation (CCE). "The new report card that we now have has sections on academic performance and co-scholastic areas. Under the co-scholastic section, a student will be graded on life skills — that is thinking, social and emotional skills and attitudes and values," Rama Sharma, CBSE spokesperson, informed mediapersons (IANS 2009). He added, "Under attitudes and values, a student's behaviour towards his or her teachers, schoolmates, toward school programmes, the environment and his or her values will be assessed and graded on a scale from A to B."

Thinking skills entail a student's capability for creative and critical thinking, social skills entail his interpersonal communication and empathy and emotional skills assess his ability to deal with stress and emotions. Just to make things clear for both students and parents, examples have been given in the report card on the parameters on which the child is being evaluated. For instance, while assessing one's social skills, such things as a student's ability to take criticism, listen to others and whether he gets along well with others, will be taken into account.

Besides these, the new report card will also be an indicator of a student's activity in the literary, scientific and aesthetic field, besides participation in school clubs and physical activity. Such a report card attempts to provide a holistic profile of the learner over a period of time.

Many in the academic field, though, are divided over whether such attributes can be graded.

There's a fear that a teacher handling 50 students may get little time to know them at an individual level, making it hard to assess their attitude. Further, subjectivity and the individual bias of the teacher may affect the assessment of a student's attitude.

Others feel that if attitudes aren't graded, they won't be taken seriously. While psychiatrist Nirmala Rao does favour the grading system, she points out that any area that is graded is taken seriously. "Unless you grade attitude, people may not pay much attention to it. At a time when there is a deterioration in a student's attitude ... grading attitude may get parents and students to take it seriously," claims Rao (Mukherji 2009).

I do see the point in providing an indicator of the students' attitudes and aptitudes. Obviously, much more than his intellectual calibre, it is his personal openness, emotional maturity and spiritual depth that really matter in the real world. Here a confidential report from peers will provide the most authentic information.

Even though there is no way we can codify and quantify attitudes, I do believe that such an attempt has to be encouraged. In a world of "vulgar salaries" and "cut throat competition," any measure that aims at deepening values and convictions of students is welcome. Should we not introduce this scheme for adults, too? And also for general public and its leaders?

45

Game, Love and Wisdom of Life

Lucian Blaga was a commanding personality in Romanian culture in the last century. He was a philosopher and writer, acclaimed for his originality, as also a university professor and diplomat. His famous poetry, "Three Faces," written in 1919, is insightful.

"The child is laughing: The Game is my wisdom and my love/ The young is singing: The Love is my wisdom and my game/ The old is silent: The Wisdom is my love and my game" (Blaga 1980). Some of his insights can be applied to our present context.

The child, with its flexibility, fantasy and spontaneity is adorable. It learns through play and gathers experiences through the innocence and transparency so unique to children. Thus, the game children play is truly a source of wisdom, love and joy. There is a sense of simplicity, trust and naiveté that makes up a child. So, Tagore could exclaim: "Every child is born with the message that God is not yet disappointed with humanity." (Clinton 1996)

As the child grows up, he or she learns to fall in love and to relish the romance of life. Love, which is much more than eroticism, makes the young optimistic and outgoing. The hope that the young nurture in the heart is a sure sign that there is so much creativity, commonality and attachment to life and to the other. Their romance may at times be blind, but they point to the fascinating and attractive dimension of life. The enthusiasm, dynamism and vitality that the young portray may at times be simplistic, but they point to life's boundless creativity. So we can very well appreciate *kama* as an intrinsic part of the Indian way of life.

When the young grow older, they look for a job, start a family and invest in things that they may not always like. An adult finds herself caught up in the daily troubles and travails of work. The routine may become enslaving. But duty calls for commitment. It is time one realised the futility of many dreams. This will make one sober and realistic, enabling that society to move ahead. It will help one sacrifice many dreams for larger causes and instil discipline so that one has a vision that is greater than oneself. This is the realm of *dharma*.

Finally, old age sets in. In spite of many setbacks and travails, most of the elderly people mature gracefully and gratefully. They learn the lessons of life, sometimes the hard way. Loss of a beloved, trials of health and failures in career give them precious insights into life. If, without bitterness, they reach out to people who have done them harm, they can really look back at life joyfully.

This is the period of "second naiveté" that philosopher Paul Ricoeur talks about. The authenticity of the aged is exhibited if they truly trust others and themselves in spite of the trials that they have experienced. It implies that despite hardships and betrayals by fellow human beings one can still love them. Is this not a foretaste of *moksha* on earth?

So, we may slightly paraphrase Lucian Blaga and chant: "The child is laughing: The Game is my wisdom, love and work/ The young is singing: The Love is my wisdom, work and game/ The adult is thinking: The Work is my wisdom, love and game./ The old is silent: The Wisdom is my love, game and work."

46

The Possibility of Impossibility

Socrates said, "Philosophy is training for dying and the task of the philosopher is to prepare for death" (Plato and Gallop 2009e). Since, for Socrates, philosophy stood for "examined life," we may rephrase him to hold that true life is about training for dying. It may sound strange for someone like Socrates, who really loved life and its ordinary pleasures.

The contemporary situation vouches for this deep insight. When we reflect further, we are struck by the paradox that most of us "live as if we never die, and die as if we have never lived." When we are alive, we behave as if we will go on living, and when confronted with the possibility of death, we panic and fret as if we never relished life!

A contemporary German philosopher, Martin Heidegger, described as the philosopher of death, holds that we are "beings-unto-death." Death is inbuilt into our very essence and every moment of our life is an anticipation of it. Even though we may not be consciously aware, death remains in the background and foreground and threatens our existence. For Heidegger, such an all-embracing death gives meaning to our existence.

For him, death is the "possibility of my impossibility" (Heidegger 1962). This possibility is at the centre of all my other possibilities, he says. There is the genuine possibility that all my possibilities will cease at the moment of death. It is this possibility that adds urgency to life and provides meaning to my limited existence, he adds.

Death makes life authentic. "As soon as man comes to life," he says, "he is at once old enough to die" (Steiner 1991).[10] Therefore, the awareness and acceptance of death is a requirement for authentic existence. Heidegger refers to the inauthentic self as the "they-self." This is the self that is influenced by the crowd or the "they," rather than by its own unique potentialities. The they-self sees death as a subject producing "cowardly fear, a sign of insecurity" and, therefore, a fit topic to be avoided.

Avoidance of death can be achieved by an evasion technique that Heidegger refers to as the "constant tranquilisation about death." In so doing, the "they-self" does not permit us the courage for anxiety in the face of death and promotes instead an "untroubled indifference" about death.

Death, the "they-self" argues, is something all human beings will experience one day in the undetermined and, therefore, easily ignored future. People experience death in the death of others, and draw conclusions about their own deaths. "One of these days one will die too; but right now it has nothing to do with us." For Heidegger, death is not a shared experience at all; rather, it is one's "ownmost" and a "non-relational" experience.

That is, death is something one can only do by oneself, as each person dies his or her own death. Death is not something that happens to other people.

What is the proper attitude towards death? Heidegger rejects the cowardly fear proposed by the "they-self." The only proper mood, he argues, when one comes "face-to-face" with the "nothing" that death reveals, is a courageous "anxiety." This anxiety or dread is different from fear in that the fear attaches to some actual object, while anxiety focuses on freedom and possibility. Only such a mood, says Heidegger, will bring about an "impassioned freedom towards death." So, death must not lead us to obsessions with morbidity, but to a sober awareness of our own possibility of impossibility (Heidegger 1962).

47

The Impossibility of Possibility

In the last article based on the German philosopher Martin Heidegger, I had spoken of death as 'the possibility of the impossibility.' In this article, I discuss the complementary position on death.

Lithuanian-French philosopher Emmanuel Lévinas was instrumental in popularising the term 'other.' For Lévinas, the 'other' is superior or prior to the self, the mere presence of the 'other' makes demands before one can respond by helping them or ignoring them.

Lévinas talks of the 'other' in terms of insomnia and wakefulness. It is an ecstasy, or exteriority toward the 'other', which forever remains beyond any attempt to capture it fully. This otherness is interminable. This 'infiniteness' of the 'other' shapes his idea of death.

Lévinas writes: "The others that obsess me in the Other do not affect me as examples of the same genus united with my neighbour by resemblance or common nature, individuations of the human race, or chips of the old block... The others concern me from the first. Here fraternity precedes the commonness of a genus. My relationship with the Other as neighbour gives meaning to my relations with all the others" (Lévinas 1998).

For Lévinas, the 'other' is not knowable and cannot be made into an object of the self, as is done by traditional metaphysics. He prefers to think of philosophy as the 'wisdom of love' rather than the love of wisdom. Here, ethical responsibility becomes integral to the subject; hence an ethics of responsibility precedes any 'objective searching after truth.'

Lévinas derives the primacy of his ethics from the experience of the encounter with the 'other'. For Lévinas, the irreducible relation, the encounter with another, is a privileged phenomenon in which the other person's proximity and distance are both strongly felt.

"The Other precisely reveals himself in his alterity not in a shock negating the I, but as the primordial phenomenon of gentleness" (Levinas 1979) 150 At the same time, the revelation of the face makes a demand, before one can realise and express one's freedom, to affirm or deny. One instantly recognises the transcendence and heteronomy of the 'other'.

Confronted with this radical otherness, Lévinas does not believe in adopting a heroic attitude toward death. Unlike Heidegger, death is never a present for Lévinas. "Death is thus never assumed, it comes." It is something that happens to us and is beyond our control. Obviously, death is related to time and our future. Lévinas claims that "Anticipation of the future and projection of the future seen as essential to time are but the present of the future and not the authentic future; the future is what is not grasped, what befalls us and lays hold of us." Thus death too falls in that category. It is 'the impossibility of having a project,' of relating to others.

Lévinas understands that if death 'opens a way out of solitude' it does so only by coming to 'crush this solitude, to crush subjectivity itself'. This leads him to look for a relationship with that which is 'other' than the self. It is our relationship with the other person that will fulfil these conditions. Death puts an end to such relationships and possibilities: the impossibility of all possibility.

In fact, our relation with death itself is a relation with "something that is absolutely other," which breaks our solitude with ourselves! Against Heidegger, Lévinas emphasises the passivity of our relationship with death.

48

Precious, But Not Precise

Sir Isaac Newton remarked once: "As a blind man has no idea of colours, so we have no idea of the manner by which the all-wise God perceives and understands all things." It is definitely a proper imagery. A blind man can be told what colour is and from his contacts with others, he can have some idea of what colour is. But he can never experience colour, as normal human beings are able to. So this assertion is a precaution and warning for all of us.

Unfortunately, many religious believers and leaders tend to make absolute claims about God and the Ultimate Reality, without taking this precaution seriously. There are many who claim to talk in the name of God, who claim to experience God and who even claim to know the mind of God. For instance, there are many who believe that God will destroy the world in 2012. There are many who dare to tell others what God wants them to do.

> We can be open to life in its fullness if we are truly aware of the present moment.

Such certitudes create dogmatism and arrogance. On the other side, a true believer humbly experiences God as the ineffable. He doesn't claim to know God's mind and dictate terms to others. He is comfortable with the mere glance of the infinite. He is grateful for the traces of God's presence that he has experienced.

To further illustrate Newton's statement, we know that we live in time and experience our world because of the forward direction of time. We also know for certain that with our death, we pass beyond the dimension of time and space. So, to speak about life after death in terms of time and space, is just like a blind man talking about colours. As limited human beings, we certainly cannot speak dogmatically of life after death, simply because life after death or nirvana is something beyond space and time.

At the same time, we just cannot hold on to Wittgenstein's dictum: "Whereof one cannot speak, thereof one must be silent" (Wittgenstein and Ogden 1990).[11] If we really follow his advice, we would not be uttering anything. Ours is a world of approximation and of inference. Even though we are not clear and certain, we ought to express ourselves. It is by such partial outward expressions that we human beings make sense of our lives and so cope with the tragedy and beauty of life.

Elaborating on the theme of life after death, most of the religious believers and mystics vouch for a life, that is more than what our "eyes have seen or ears heard." This, too, is a beautiful allegorical expression, which is inadequate and at the same time necessary.

Yet, the paradox should be noted. A genuine mystical experience is definitely more certain and life transforming than all other empirical experiences. For a mystic, who has at least once heard the call of God directly and experienced the divine presence at least for a few moments, everything else become secondary. So, every true religious believer must acknowledge the genuineness and authenticity of mystical experiences.

We need to keep a balance between these two levels. A mystic may genuinely speak of God and ultimate reality with full conviction and definitiveness. But these words are like a blind man describing the beauty and richness of colour. So, we should not be dogmatic about our religious words and experiences. Nor should we disparage them. They are not precise, but they are precious. They are not absolute but are the greatest that we humans possess. For, we are both frail and great.

49

The Power of the Present

Many spiritual masters urge us to live in the present. The main reason for our present suffering is inordinately clinging to the past or planning for the future. Being present to the present, they say, makes us attentive and opens us to the joy of living.

One such writer is the best-selling author Eckhart Tolle. He is said to have attained enlightenment at the age of 29 "after suffering long periods of depression, dissolving his old identity and radically changing the course of his life." Tolle's bestseller, "The Power of Now" (Tolle 2004) emphasizes the importance of being aware of the present moment as a way of not being lost in thought. According to him, the present is the gateway to a heightened sense of peace and aliveness. "Being in the now" also brings about an awareness that is beyond the mind. This awareness helps us in transcending "the pain-body" that is created by the identification of the mind and ego with the body. His later book, "A New Earth" (Tolle 2005) further explores the structure of the human ego and how this acts to distract people from their present experience of the world.

With the aim of transforming the individual and the collective human consciousness, in other words, for a global spiritual awakening Tolle teaches the following:

1. We are not our thoughts. We are the awareness behind them. Thoughts are often negative and painful. However, the thoughts are not us, although our ego wants us to think so. Awareness of

our thoughts without being caught up in them is the first step to freedom.

2. Only the present moment exists. That is where life is (indeed it is the only place life can truly be found). Becoming aware of the 'now' has the added benefit that it will draw our attention away from our (negative) thoughts. Use mindfulness techniques to fully appreciate our surroundings and everything we are experiencing. Look and listen intently. Give full attention to the smallest details.

3. Accept the present moment. It is resistance to the present moment that creates most of the difficulties in our life. However, acceptance does not mean that we cannot take action to rectify the situation we are in. What is important is to drop resistance so that we let the moment be, and that any action arises from a deeper awareness rather than from resistance. Much of the pain in a person's life comes from resistance to what is.

4. Observe the pain-body. Years of conditioned thought patterns, individually and collectively, have resulted in habitual emotional reactions with an apparent personality of their own. During 'pain-body attacks' we become completely identified with this 'pain identity' and respond from its agenda – which is to create more pain for ourselves and others. Observing the pain-body is awareness itself – as it allows humans to separate from this unconscious identification with pain.

It may be added that the "pain-body" mentioned above is the cause both of pain and of pleasure. Such a body opens us to experience both the struggles of daily life and the bliss of normal life. As such the "pain-body" need not be seen as a derogatory term, but part of our being human.

Thus, it becomes clear that focusing on the 'now' or being totally attentive to the present enables us to be attentive to life. We can be open to life in its fullness if we are truly aware of the present moment.

50

Longevity and Personality Traits

Researchers from Boston University School have found that specific personality traits are associated with healthy aging and longevity. The findings of their work, conducted in collaboration with scientists from the National Institute on Aging, appear on-line in the Journal of the *American Geriatrics Society* (Boston_University 2009).

Previous research on children and relatives of very elderly people have shown that exceptional longevity runs strongly in families. Studies of the offspring of centenarians showed that their mortality is 120 percentage lower than other members of their birth group and that they also have markedly lower prevalence rates and delayed onsets of cardiovascular disease, hypertension, and diabetes mellitus. Because personality traits have been shown to have substantial heritable components, the researchers hypothesized that certain personality features may be important to the healthy aging observed in the offspring of centenarians.

They based their study on the "Big Five" factors of personality or five broad domains or dimensions of personality which are used to describe human personality. It measures the personality traits for openness, conscientiousness, extraversion, agreeableness and neuroticism (Wikipedia_contributors 2012).

Openness - (inventive / curious vs. cautious / conservative). It indicates appreciation for art, emotion, adventure, unusual ideas, curiosity and a variety of experience. Conscientiousness - (efficient

/ organized vs. easy-going / careless). It has a tendency to show self-discipline, act dutifully and aim for achievement; planned rather than spontaneous behaviour.

> It is up to us make a difference, even a minor one, in our community and take it forward spiritually.

Extraversion - (outgoing / energetic vs. shy / withdrawn). It implies energy, positive emotions, urgency, and the tendency to seek stimulation in the company of others.

Agreeableness - (friendly / compassionate vs. competitive / outspoken). It is a tendency to be compassionate and cooperative rather than suspicious and antagonistic towards others.

Neuroticism - (sensitive / nervous vs. secure /confident) denotes a tendency to experience unpleasant emotions easily, such as anger, anxiety, depression, or vulnerability.

The survey was conducted on 246 unrelated offsprings of centenarians with an average age of 75. Both the male and female offspring of centenarians scored in the low range of published norms for neuroticism and in the high range for extraversion. The women also scored comparatively high in agreeableness. Otherwise, both sexes scored within normal range for conscientiousness and openness, and the men scored within normal range for agreeableness (Boston_University 2009).

According to the researchers, personality traits in the offspring of centenarians appear to have distinctive characteristics that may have important implications for their longevity. Interestingly, whereas men and women generally differ substantially in their personality characteristics, the male and female offspring of centenarians tended to be similar, which speaks to the importance of these traits, irrespective of gender, for health, aging and longevity.

"It's likely that the low neuroticism and higher extraversion will confer health benefits for these subjects," said senior author Thomas Perls, director of the New England Centenarian Study (Boston_University 2009). For instance, "people who are lower in neuroticism are able to manage or regulate stressful situations more effectively than those with higher neuroticism levels. Similarly, high extraversion levels have been associated with establishing friendships and looking after yourself," he said, as reported in Science Daily (Boston_University 2009). These findings suggest that personality is "an important characteristic to include in studies that assess genetic and environmental determinants of longevity."

Though longevity itself is not a measure of spiritual growth, improvement in personality traits definitely is. As one grows in healthy spirituality, one is expected to be comparatively more open, agreeable and extravert. In this sense, there would be a correlation between healthy spirituality and longevity. People who can cope with tension better, who can laugh at themselves heartily and get along better are comparatively more spiritual – not compared to other humans but to their own older selves.

51

Making a Minor Difference

Good acts – those of kindness, generosity and cooperation — multiply just as easily as bad. And it takes only a handful of individuals to really make a difference for the good. In a study published in the online edition of the *Proceedings of the National Academy of Sciences*, researchers from the University of California, San Diego and Harvard provide the first laboratory evidence that cooperative behaviour is transmittable and that it spreads from person to person to person. When people benefit from kindness they "pay it forward" by helping others who were not originally involved, and this creates a cascade of cooperation that influences dozens more in a social network.

James Fowler and Nicholas Christakis offered these insights in their book *Connected: The Surprising Power of Our Social Networks and How They Shape Our Lives* (Christakis and Fowler 2009). In the study, the authors show that when one person gives money to help others in a "public-goods game," where people have the opportunity to cooperate with each other, the recipients are more likely to give their own money away to other people in future games. This creates a domino effect in which one person's generosity spreads first to three people and then to the nine people that those three people interact with in the future, and then to still other individuals in subsequent waves of the experiment.

The effect persists, Fowler said: "You don't go back to being your 'old selfish self.'' As a result, the money a person gives in the first round of the experiment is ultimately tripled by others who are subsequently (directly or indirectly) influenced to give more.

"Though the multiplier in the real world may be higher or lower than what we've found in the lab," Fowler said, "personally it's very exciting to learn that kindness spreads to people I don't know or have never met. We have direct experience of giving and seeing people's immediate reactions, but we don't typically see how our generosity cascades through the social network to affect the lives of dozens or maybe hundreds of other people" (University_of_California_San_Diego 2010).

The study participants were strangers to each other and never played twice with the same person, a study design that eliminates direct reciprocity and reputation management as possible causes. The study is the first one to document experimentally their earlier findings that social contagion travels in networks up to three degrees of separation, and the first to corroborate evidence from others' observational studies on the spread of cooperation.

The contagious effect in the study was symmetric; uncooperative behaviour also spread, but there was nothing to suggest that it spread any more or any less robustly than cooperative behaviour, Fowler said.

From a scientific perspective, Fowler added, these findings suggest the fascinating possibility that the process of contagion may have contributed to the evolution of cooperation: Groups with altruists in them will be more altruistic as a whole and more likely to survive than selfish groups.

> "The flow of good and desirable properties like ideas, love and kindness is required for human social networks to endure, and, in turn, networks are required for such properties to spread. Humans form social networks because the benefits of a connected life outweigh the costs"

"Our work over the past few years, examining the function of human social networks and their genetic origins, has led us to conclude that there is a deep and fundamental connection between social networks and goodness," said Christakis. "The flow of good and desirable properties like ideas, love and kindness is required for human social networks to endure, and, in turn, networks are required for such properties to spread. Humans form social networks because the benefits of a connected life outweigh the costs" (University_of_California_San_Diego 2010).

So networking and social connectedness is inevitable and fosters good or evil. It is up to us make a difference, even a minor one, in our community and take it forward spiritually and morally.

52

Antony Flew: A Searching Philosopher

Antony Flew, an academic philosopher, who expounded atheism for most of his life but made a late conversion to belief in a creator, died on April 8, 2010. The son of a Methodist minister, Flew abandoned belief as a teenager because of the problem of evil. "It just seemed flatly inconsistent to say that the universe was created by an omnipotent and perfectly good being. Yet there were evils in abundance which could not be put down to a consequence of human sin," he was quoted as saying in a 2004 interview with The Sunday Times.

Always describing himself as a "negative atheist," he asserted that "theological propositions can neither be verified nor falsified by experience," a position he expounded in his classic paper "Theology and Falsification" (1950), reputedly the most frequently-quoted philosophical publication of the second half of the 20th century (Flew 2000).

After years of fighting against theists, when Flew revealed that he had come to the conclusion that there might be a God after all, it came as a shock to his fellow atheists, who had long regarded him as one of their foremost champions. Worse, he seemed to have deserted Plato for Aristotle, since it was two of Aquinas's famous five proofs for the existence of God – the arguments from design and for a prime mover – that had apparently clinched the matter.

After months of soul-searching, Flew concluded that research into DNA had "shown, by the almost unbelievable complexity of the arrangements which are needed to produce life, that intelligence must have been involved." Moreover, though he accepted Darwinian evolution, he felt that it could not explain the beginnings of life. "I have been persuaded that it is simply out of the question that the first living matter evolved out of dead matter and then developed into an extraordinarily complicated creature," he said.

Regarding the origin of life, he pointed out "the improbable statistics involved and the pure chances that have to occur. It's simply not on to think this could occur simply by chance," he told the "The Sunday Times" in 2004 (Associated_Press 2010).

Unlike traditional theists', Flew's conversion did not embrace such concepts as Heaven, good and evil or the afterlife – let alone divine intervention in human affairs. His belief was in deism, in a remote creator who takes no interest in human affairs. Flew said he was impressed by the work of Gerard Schroeder, a physicist and Jewish theologian who wrote "The Hidden Face of God," where the living God prefers to remain hidden (Schroeder 2001).

Flew's volte-face on the existence of God was all the more remarkable given the volume of his writing for the atheistic cause and his vehement denial of internet rumours in 2001 that he had renounced his atheism. His response was entitled *Sorry to Disappoint, but I'm Still an Atheist!* In 2007, however, he published "There is a God: How the World's Most Notorious Atheist Changed his Mind" (Flew and Varghese 2007).

So even the theist Flew is quite categorical: "I don't want a future life." He added, "I want to be dead when I'm dead and that's an end to it. I don't want an unending life. I don't want anything without end."

As a person and philosopher, he was always questioning and searching. He posed uncomfortable questions without always finding answers. His intellectual integrity led him to accept an unconventional God. His life reminds us that may be posing the question is more important than finding the answer, provided we are honest about it. Our integrity and honesty will lead us to untrodden and fulfilling paths. Maybe being on the way is our human destiny.

Wealth and Wisdom

53

Market, Religion and Sense of Fairness

Human behaviours are often explained as hard-wired evolutionary leftovers of life on the Savannah or during the Stone Age. But a study of one very modern behaviour, fairness towards total strangers, suggests it evolved recently, and is rooted more in culture rather than genetics. In other words, cultural DNA, encouraged by market and religion fostered a sense of fairness.

> "What we lack is not food but justice"

In a series of three behavioural tests given to 2,100 people, an innate sense of fairness was shown to evolve by participation in complex market and religious structures. Generally speaking, these use social norms and informal institutions to promote fairness.

Genetically speaking, people in the study weren't different from their 200,000 BC ancestors. What was different was their cultural DNA. "You can't get the effects we're seeing from genes," said Joe Henrich, a University of British Columbia evolutionary psychologist and co-author of the study, published in *Science* (Keim 2010).

Kindness towards strangers is a baffling human trait, given that strangers appear to have been treated with suspicion and violence for most of human history. Some analyses of mortality in the Stone Age estimate that one in seven people died in violent combats. But something changed. Small, family-based groups came together, forming hunter-gatherer tribes. With the advent of agriculture, tribes gave way to city-states. Then came nations. Anthropologists say all this was only possible because people were willing to treat total strangers with fairness reserved for kin.

Henrich's team thinks that fairness between strangers at the individual level is what allows social organisms to thrive, and to out-compete more selfish societies.

"Once you get cultural evolution going with any strength, you get enforcement of these norms." Behaviours interlock in a way that rewards fairness and punishes its violation.

To study this dynamics, Henrich's team had 2,100 people — hunter-gatherers, marine foragers, pastoralists, horticulturalists and wage labourers — play three variations of a game designed to measure their innate sense of fairness. When people lived in larger communities, and participated more in markets and religion, they were more willing to share, and punish selfishness.

In smaller communities, people have narrow concepts of fairness, "But they're not for dealing with people outside your sphere. There are no default norms for that. There are norms for fairness, but not the kind that let you build a large, well-running culture," Henrich said (Keim 2010).

"These findings call into question the standard assumption in economics that preferences are innate and stable," wrote Karla Hoff, a World Bank economist. Henrich suggests that culture evolved towards fairness for hundreds of thousands of years before the advent of agriculture, which in turn fostered stable, ever-larger community structures.

"We can't rule out the possibility that there was culture-gene interaction, but all the variation we see could be explained by plain cultural evolution," Henrich reports in Wired magazine (Keim 2010). If these findings are true, market dynamics and religious structures have positively contributed to the evolution of a sense of fairness. So market, culture and religion may be intimately intertwined to give us a sense of justice.

54

Abolish Poverty to Attain Spirituality

Poverty around us and spirit within us are related. Without alleviating poverty, it is hypocritical to talk of being spiritual and moral. All of us can, in our own little way, help in this process by taking action to raise awareness among people about the causes for poverty and participate in global conversations about the critical issues facing our generation.

To collectively face the problem of hunger and malnutrition, more than 173 million people smashed the Guinness world record for largest human mobilisation when they gathered in October 2009 at over 3,000 events in more than 120 countries to demand that their governments eliminate extreme poverty and achieve the millennium development goals (MDGs) set by the United Nations.

So far, this year's record is held by the global campaign "Stand Up, Take Action, End Poverty Now!" In 2006, 23 million people stood up. In 2007, 47 million people stood up. In 2008, 116 million people stood up and took action. The mobilisation was organised globally by the United Nations Millennium Campaign (UNMC) in partnership with the Global Call to Action Against Poverty. "The more than 173 million people who mobilised [in 2009] sent a clear message to world leaders that there is massive, universal, global demand for eradicating poverty," said Salil Shetty, head of the UNMC (OneWorld 2009).

There's an online campaign, too, which was officially launched worldwide in different parts of the world. The partnership brings together high-profile speakers to discuss poverty with citizens around the world in 30-minute interactive online conversations. Several of these discussions are recorded and include talks by Grammy award-winning singer Angelique Kidjo, who spoke with the youth in Uganda about education, and award-winning Nigerian singer Femi Kuti, who spoke with school children in Kenya about poverty. In fact, anyone can join the conversation about poverty and its root causes on these powerful social networking platforms (Grandia 2009).

There events happening off-line as well. Celebrities and ordinary citizens are coming together on social networking sites to participate and engage in live discussions with world leaders and decision makers.

The mobilisation in 2009 gave particular emphasis to telling world leaders that their track record on women's rights, maternal mortality and hunger is unacceptable. Citizens refuse to accept the fact that 70 per cent of the people living in poverty are women and children and 500,000 women continue to die annually in the process of giving birth, and are demanding urgent action from their leaders (Grandia 2009).

It is ironical that we have the technological resources to feed everyone and to end world hunger, but "what we lack is not food but justice," say some participants. So, in effect, what is in short supply is spiritual hunger that cannot rest unless we feed everyone physically and emotionally. In fact, the tragedy of our world is that both the overfed and the undernourished are unhappy. Only when we learn to live with each other, respect ourselves and share the resources equitably and fairly, will we – both the rich and the poor – be satisfied in the true sense.

In fact the tragedy of our world is that both the over-fed and the under-nourished are unhappy. Only when we learn to live with each other, respect ourselves and share the resources equitably and fairly, will we – both the rich and the poor – satisfied. So the stand we take to end poverty is in fact a stand for our own spiritual dignity and moral depth. For only through spirituality and morality can we abolish poverty. Without alleviating poverty, it is hypocritical to talk of being spiritual and moral. That precisely was Mahatma Gandhi's vision!

55

Towards 'Zero Hunger' Programme

As the United Nations food agency met in Rome to discuss ways to combat global hunger, Brazil could tout the success of the country's "Zero Hunger" program. While the country still faces major challenges, including massive economic disparities, the UN Food and Agriculture Organization (FAO) estimates malnutrition has been reduced by 73 percent in the last six years and infant mortality by 45 percentage in the same period.

The "Zero Hunger" programme began in 2003, combining dozens of social programs ranging from the construction of water tanks in dry regions to agricultural loans and food aid. Key to the efforts has been the "Family Purse" programme, which has been adopted in several African and Latin American countries. The program allots 55 dollars a month to poor families on the condition their children go to school, and distributes food to some 37 million children while they are at school. Today, some 12.4 million families are part of the Family Purse program, around a quarter of the country's 190 million residents.

Can the poor dream of a zero-hunger situation?

Brazil's efforts have won praise from the FAO and created interest abroad. "We hope that at the end of the FAO summit, when the presidents and prime ministers return to their home countries, they will launch their own 'Zero Hunger' programmes and help other countries do the same," said Andrew Macmillan, former director of the FAO's operations department.

"Between 2003 and 2008, the proportion of people living in poverty in Brazil has gone from 28 percent to 16 percent. That means that 19.3 million people have moved out of poverty," said Marcelo Neri, head of the Center for Social policies at the Getulio Vargas Foundation. Brazil, like India, is a massive food producer with large areas of arable land.

Coming to our Indian situation two experts on poverty have come up with new research, which shows that India's high economic growth since 1991 is, indeed, pro-poor and has decisively reduced poverty. Gaurav Datt and Martin Ravallion, both respected economists, employed a new series of consumption-based poverty measures from 1950 to 2006 and 47 rounds of National Sample Surveys, to show that slightly more than one person in two lived below the poverty line in India during the 1950s and '60s. By 1990 this had fallen to one person in three. By 2005, it fell again, and only one in five persons now lives below the poverty line. By the criterion of consumption the poverty ratio or the number of poor as a percentage of total population in India for 2004-05 is estimated at 37.2 per cent, according to a new report submitted by the Suresh Tendulkar.

In their paper "Has India's Economic Growth Become More Pro-Poor in the Wake of Economic Reforms?" the authors conclude that "the post-reform process of urban economic growth has brought significant gains to the rural poor as well as the urban poor." The poor in urban and rural areas are now linked through trade, migration and transfers, which explains why rising standards in India's towns are helping to reduce poverty in the villages. Even though agricultural growth has been relatively weak since 1991, overall high growth has positively affected the lives of the rural masses.

This happy news on growth, however, must be seen in the context of lost opportunities. In another study comparing India, China and Brazil, Martin Ravallion shows that China (with higher growth) and Brazil (with lower growth) have done a much better job at poverty reduction. If only India could reform agriculture and had functioning schools and health centres, the poor could dream of a zero-hunger situation. Then we can address the problem of our collective spiritual hunger.

56

The Irrelevance of Budget

Presenting the annual budget and making glowing or censorious reviews of it has become a regular feature of our Indian democracy. TV channels and newspaper industry flourish on it. In historical terms, the annual Budget is a relatively new invention. Its origins, however, lie in our connection to the British Raj and in centuries of their rulers mismanaging the country's finances.

In 1870, the then chancellor of Britain, Robert Lowe, described his office in these terms: "The chancellor of the exchequer is a man whose duties make him more or less of a taxing machine. He is entrusted with a certain amount of misery which it is his duty to distribute as fairly as he can." Presenting the Indian budget may not such a thankless affair.

In spite of the raving reviews that the budget gets, it is worthwhile to ask some significant questions: does it really matter? Does it change the lives of the people, especially the really poor? Has it not become a meaningless ritual?

Consider all the New Year resolutions that we have made! All the birthday wishes that we have received! Have they really made any significant contribution to our well-being? Except for our own emotional satisfaction, do they contribute objectively to our well-being and growth?

The considered response, I believe, is ambivalent. Of course the new year resolutions do change me – to a very limited extent. At least it changes me to the extent I take some trouble to prioritise my goal and articulate them. Further it gives me a measuring rod to find out where I have gone wrong!

But in a nation, where about four hundred million people go hungry even after sixty years of planned economy and supposed implementation of five year plans, it is easy to become cynical. It is easy to point out the stifling effects of our bureaucracy especially on the poor. One can go on criticizing the corrupt system and politicians who are ingenuous to go beyond any norms or laws imposed by budgetary regulations or legal challenges. One can point out that without walking the talk, budget loses its teeth, however liberating its proposals may be!

Still, without blindly absolutising the budget, we must point out that it is a symbol of the collective vision of the Indian nation and outline priorities which may be implemented. After all the eulogies and denigration meted out to the budgetary proposals, one can still use it as a measuring rod – that measures both our collective failures and successes.

As individuals and society, we need to realize that everything in life cannot be planned and determined. Many a times, things cannot be predicted nor controlled. The old deterministic or linear way of life just does not hold for human life. Complete chaos is not the answer. So today scholars talk of "chaordic" system where we need a balance between chaos and order or between planning and flexibility. Only in such an ambience can life, creativity and love flourish.

Budget can be critiqued and commended upon, depending on my perspective and vision. But we must at the same time be proud of the fact that as a nation, we have been able to propose a budget to ourselves. Something that many individual Indians are unfortunately incapable of doing!

The railway minister quoted our national poet Tagore while presenting the budget. In the same vein, our budget can be relevant only "where the mind is without fear and the head is held high" and only if we collectively and creatively commit ourselves to our land and pray in the words of Tagore: "into that heaven of freedom, my Father, let my country awake."

57

Faith and Suffering

The key Buddhist insight into our suffering is intimately linked with religion. All religions attempt to respond to the suffering we experience every day. And all religions try to reduce or even eliminate suffering. The believer is given guidance and direction to cope with suffering. He is also given the assurance that his suffering is not in vain. In this sense, suffering is given meaning and, thus, made bearable by religion.

> Any small act that we do as individuals to foster equality and respect enables human agents to realise their own capability and freedom.

At the same time, it is unfortunate that individuals who are peace-loving can cause havoc when they come together. So "man is good, men are bad." Religions, especially organised religions, have given rise to atrocities, even in the name of God.

That is why Sam Harris, in his book, "The End of Faith: Religion, Terror and the Future of Reason," used September 11 as an example to show that "religious faith is the single greatest threat to the survival of the human species today" (Harris 2005). He even maintains that killing people who believe in God just for that belief is ethical. "Some propositions are so dangerous that it may even be ethical to kill people for believing them," he says.

Scholars such as Richard Dawkins, Daniel Dennett, Christopher Hitchens continue to maintain that religion is the cause of all the world's ills. They forget the fact that if religion is wiped out, humans will invent something more powerful to give vent to their evil inclination. Mao Tse Tung, Josef Stalin, Vladimir Lenin and Adolf Hitler all promoted a religion-less utopia and murdered over 100 million people in their attempt to produce it — far beyond the religious killing done in the crusades, inquisition and witch trials.

Going beyond organised religions and discovering one's personal, individualised religion is also no answer to the problem of our collective suffering. When I have no higher power to answer to and to draw inspiration from, ethics becomes a function of the beliefs of the human powers that be. A privatised spirituality that ignores organised religion cannot really make the world more peaceful.

Given the interdependent nature of our existence in today's globalised world, we need a structure that will promote harmony, peace and fairness. Gone are the days when individuals could come up with solutions for humanity. Today we need concerted collective efforts to usher in peace. Unfortunately, organised religions have failed. So have nation-states.

But there is still a lot of vigour and vitality in religions, including in the organised ones, to foster fellowship among the diverse peoples of the world. Religions have been the motivating force to do good even to those who do evil.

Modern atheist attacks give sweeping generalities that are unfortunate distortions of what is true and what will work. So, one of the fiercest critics of religion, the atheist Bertrand Russell, could hold: "Although the great majority of Christians failed lamentably in Christian charity, the ideal remained alive and in every age inspired some notable saints." The same is applicable to all religions. In fact, Gilbert K. Chesterton is right: "Christianity has not been tried and found wanting; it has been found difficult and not tried" (Chesterton 2007).

The world needs to rediscover true religions. In this common search to eliminate suffering and foster peace, people of all religions and of no religion, hopefully, can come together.

58

Amartya Sen: Defining the Nature of a Just Society

The Theory of Justice is the most important contribution of Nobel laureate Amartya Sen (Sen 2009). Most modern philosophers are concerned with finding the right rules, institutions and social contracts for a just society. This school of thought dubbed as "transcendental institutionalism" by Sen, found its greatest 20th-century exponent in John Rawls. Rawls' *The Idea of Justice* (Rawls 2005) was built on Kant and Rousseau.

Sen characterises the transcendental institutionalists as engaged in a "long-range search for perfectly just institutions," and a hunt for "spotless justice." The transcendental theory of justice flourished in the Enlightenment and has proponents among some of the most distinguished philosophers of our day; it is concerned with identifying perfectly just social arrangements, defining the nature of the perfectly just society.

So, if removing injustice is the goal, then starting with the question "what constitutes perfect justice?," as many main mainstream theories of justice do, seems misguided. For Sen, these philosophies are ultimately regressive, because societies are, in fact, full of actual human beings and will never agree on a final, perfect set of institutions and rules.

Sen quotes Bernard Williams: "Disagreement does not necessarily have to be overcome." He opines that the search for perfect justice can distract us from tackling real life, immediate injustices such as access to education for women in the developing world or action on climate change. The perfect becomes the enemy of the good. Therefore, he argues for a comparative perspective on justice. Focusing on the comparative judgments of what is "more" or "less" just, and on the comparative merits of the different societies that actually emerge from certain institutions and social interactions, enables us to implement programmes that make our society more equal. The "comparative" approach examines "what kind of lives people can actually lead."

Abolishing slavery or giving women the right to vote would free people to lead lives of their own choosing, even without creating a perfectly just society, says Sen. The keystone of judging the lives people can actually lead is an assessment of what he has labelled their "capabilities" — or, as he explains, "the power to do something."

Sen thinks that national rural employment guarantee act (NREGA) of India has basically done a lot of good in the country. He is frustrated that people do one good thing but neglect the other side. In order to evaluate NREGA, we can ask: Has it been able to reach a lot of people who would have otherwise not been reached? Has it increased the income levels of some and thus provided some level of security and been able to tackle to some extent the problem of undernourishment, Sen's unambiguous answer is: Yes.

But the problem of widespread undernourishment continues to be a real blot on India's record. Therefore, the discussion and action on right to food and on employment guarantee is crucial. Reaching the undernourished people of the world is difficult and, in India, it's challenging, and for that we have to attack it on many fronts.

Taking the cue from Sen, we can hold that any small act that we do as individuals to foster equality and respect enables human agents to realise their own capability and freedom. This leads to situations that are more just. Without it we cannot meaningfully speak of spiritual depth and transparency.

Self and Security

59

Try to Be True to Your Own Self

"The greatest tragedy of life is to spend your whole life fishing only to discover that it was not fish you were after," wrote Henry David Thoreau. Unfortunately, this is true of many of us. What separates those who live well and die happy from others is that they continually asked themselves whether they were living the life they wanted to and were following their heart.

> Can we live the wisdom treasured in our traditions?

If we are to follow our hearts and be true to ourselves, we must make the choice to live our life consciously. As exhorted by Greek philosopher Socrates, we need to live an examined life. Unless we are continuously examining our lives to make sure that it is on target, there is a very good chance that we will end up living someone else's life.

In an interview conducted by American doctor John Izzo, a 72-year old woman was asked to advise younger people how to find happiness and purpose. Her answer was insightful. "I cannot do that. In order to tell a person the secret to happiness, I would have to sit down with them, look them deeply in the eyes, find out who they are, find out what their dreams are. I say this because the secret to happiness is to be true to your self" (Izzo 2008).

Three guiding questions that will help us to examine if we are living lives true to ourselves are: One, am I following my heart and being true to myself? Two, is my life focused on the things that really matter to me? And three, am I being the person I want to be in the world?

Often the seeds of not being true to our own selves begin very early in our lives, when we begin to compare ourselves with others. A young student would pick up a student every year and would tell him, "I want to be like him." Enlightenment came to him after many years, when he realised that he was not any of those boys. The path to happiness was not in deciding which one he wanted to be like, but to decide what was most true to him.

Being true to ourselves and following our hearts requires tremendous courage. It implies quieting other voices that may want us to follow their dream. Being true to oneself often involves hearing the one voice that calls us, even if others cannot hear it. So, to be true to ourselves, we need to cultivate the discipline to listen to ourselves and have the courage to follow it. The discipline to listen means setting time aside to ask important questions about ourselves, unlike many others who hardly have time to hear the voices of their own souls. To have the courage to follow the inner voice implies that we resolutely, firmly and lovingly say no to some of the offers and choose others, even though they may not be that convenient or comfortable.

A 71-year-old physics professor has evaluated the students he taught for 40 years and summed it up: "There is a chasm of difference between those students who were following their hearts and those that were not." Those who studied physics because of other compulsions struggled. The others "following their hearts worked through the challenges. Years later, I would meet many of these students, and those who followed their heart continued to do well, while those who had not seemed to struggle their entire lives.

A happy and purposeful life makes us wise and authentic. In the final analysis, we are accountable to ourselves. When we are true to ourselves, we are true to others and to God.

60

Five Secrets You Must Discover

Award-winning author, corporate culture crusader and an advocate of global sustainability, John B. Izzo, has written an extraordinary book on attaining and living wisdom. His approach is purely experimental. He asked about 15,000 people to send him names of people who are considered to be wise. The questions posed to them were: Who are the wise elders in your life? Do you know of someone who has lived a long time and has something important to teach us about living?

Of the 1,000 suggestions that he received, he narrowed down his choice through pre-interviews to 235 people who were acknowledged as wise.

Izzo's team conducted one-to-three hour interviews with all these 235 wise men and women. Some of the questions posed to them were: What brought you the greatest happiness? What are your regrets? What mattered and what turned out not to matter in life? What do you wish you had learned earlier?

The findings were tabulated, televised and summed up in a book entitled: *The Five Secrets You Must Discover Before You Die* (Izzo 2008). The book found two profound insights. First, it found that there were many real "secrets" in our lives. What the author discovered was that there were indeed secrets that these people discover and thus live a more meaningful life. Secrets, which, in fact, are obvious to many of us, but we do not really live them.

The second insight in the title, "Before You Die," reminds us that there is some urgency to discovering what really matters. Many of the friends of the author thought that having the word "die" in the title of the book was depressing. Some others felt that it was necessary, since it lets the reader know the urgency of discovering what really matters.

The first secret is being true to oneself. The second one is leaving no regrets. The third one is to love. The next one is to live the moment. The final secret found in almost all these people was giving to life more than one took.

The insight on these five secrets, the author believes, is for people at every stage of life. It is a book for young people who are just starting out on the journey of life. Just as young people, who are internet-savvy, use it to tap the experiences of others with products, the experiences of these 235 people concerning things that matter in their lives can be tapped by others. In this manner, we will enrich ourselves, whether we are young or old.

In the first chapter, the author begins by asking: Why do some people find meaning and die happy? It is because they know the secrets and have found the wisdom to live accordingly. The secrets discovered and discussed are not radically new, rather they are so universally common among diverse groups of people who have found happiness and purpose. In this sense Leo Tolstoy is right when he asserts that "happy families are all alike; but an unhappy family is unhappy in its own way."

As human beings living in this present time of unparalleled technological growth and economic prosperity, and as a human family, we have really no reason to be unhappy. The amount of knowledge available to us has been exponentially growing for the past two hundred years. The religious therapies and spiritual insights available to us is unparalleled. Yet, we, both as individuals and society, manage to remain unhappy and depressed. This is not because we lack knowledge but because we dare not to live the wisdom treasured in our traditions and found in many of our elders and wise people around us.

61

A Life Without Any Regrets

The bitterest tears shed over graves are for words left unsaid and deeds left undone, proclaimed author Harriet Beecher Stowe. Regret is possibly one thing we all fear the most; that we might look back on our lives and wish that we had done things differently.

In fact, it is said that what we fear most is not death, but not having lived to the fullest extent possible, to come to the end of our life with our final words being, "I wish I had..." Therefore, to find happiness and purpose in life, we must embrace the secret of not leaving any regrets. For this, we must live with courage, moving toward what we want rather than away from what we fear. To leave no regrets, we must face and befriend the inevitable disappointments that life hands over to us.

> Can we live the wisdom treasured in our traditions?

Every choice involves giving up something and taking risks. At the end of our lives, we will not regret the risks we took and failed. It is the experience of most people that they do not take enough risks.

Knowing that we will likely regret the thing we did not try can have a significant effect on how we make decisions. Failure, according to businessman John Lizzo, is not the regret that haunts most people; it is the choice not to risk failure at all (Izzo 2008).

So, we must make the basic choice of whether we will live in fear or focus on what we want to achieve. Each time we play safe, we move farther away from our truest self and plant the seeds of future regret.

A lady had six unfinished books waiting to be completed. When asked for the reason, she was frank: "All of my life, I have left things unfinished. I thought it was just procrastination. But as I reflect on it, I believe I have not finished these books because if I ever do finish them, I would have to let someone read them. And if I let someone read them, perhaps they will tell me that I cannot write. I suppose it is the fear of rejection that has kept me from finishing."

In fact, many of us do the same things. For fear of rejection or failure, or because we are not sure that we will succeed, we die with our books, our dreams, our story inside us.

On the other side, we must realise that our lives can never be without some regrets. Regret does serve an important positive function: it reminds us of what really matters. And we listen to regrets, as they can keep us from the deeper pool of regret and depression that may lie ahead.

But, if we regularly check in with the older version of ourselves, we are less likely to leave undone that which we are called to do. So, the minor regrets that all of us have can motivate us to live in such a way now so that we do not have to face the major regrets concerning the basic nature of our lives.

Here are four sets of questions that will enable us to live without deep regrets: One, did I act out of fear today? How do I want to be more proactive tomorrow? Two, did I act on my convictions today? How do I want to act on them more deeply tomorrow? Three, what step would I take in my life right now if I were acting with courage, not fear? What might I do differently right now if I were living from the perspective of an old person looking back at my life? Four, how am I responding to the setbacks in my life right now? Am I stepping forward or retreating?

62

Relationships Are Key to Happiness

The Dalai Lama advises us, "If you want others to be happy, practice compassion. If you want to be happy, practice compassion." In fact, when we reach the evening of our lives, it is only compassion, love and relationships that are meaningful. In fact, love is the greatest source of happiness and of regret for most people, when they look back on life.

Most of us commonly perceive love as an emotion. When it is about things that really matter, love goes beyond emotion and becomes a choice. Though we may not always "feel" love towards another, we can always choose to love him or her.

Mother Teresa could hold the hands of a leprosy patient and look at him lovingly. It is because, though she does not feel like loving a leper, she had the power "to choose to love this man." She could instantly see the beauty within the apparently wretched man.

To love and to become a loving person, we must first choose to love ourselves. Unless we fundamentally choose to see ourselves as worthy, we cannot love others. The love of oneself is fundamental to being a spiritually healthy person.

Elsa, a victim of World War II, was abandoned by her father and unloved by her mother. One day, after prolonged self-doubt and pity, she came to a realisation. "At one moment, I realised that if I could not get love, I had to 'become love'. It is hard to explain, but what I realised was that while I had very little control over whether others loved me, I realised that I had complete control over whether

I became a loving person." She added, "Somehow I knew that if I became a loving person, people could not help but love me." So, genuine transformation can occur when I decide to "become love rather than to seek love."

Researcher John Izzo asked old and fulfilled people what their greatest source of happiness was (Izzo 2008). They would most of the time refer to spouses, children, parents and friends. "Again and again, I saw that people who focus on the development of deep personal relationships in their lives become happy." Thus choosing to act with love toward those closest to us and making loving relationships a priority in our lives enable us to live wise and fulfilled lives.

Then there is need to actualise our love in day-to-day dealings with the people we meet. Actually, rather than wait for the "great moments of love," it is easier to do little acts of kindness. Smiling at others, speaking warmly to someone, being there for a friend when he or she needs us may look unimportant, but these are key moments of our 'becoming love'. Making a stranger feel at home or visiting a sick person transforms us. They make us more sensitive and compassionate.

Izzo is convinced: "Although we have little control over whether we get love, we have almost complete control over whether we become love." He adds, "The people I spoke to had made a conscious choice to become love in their lives and, in the process, they found happiness."

It is not primarily receiving love that matters. Nor does the feeling of love matter much. But we can become love and, in the process, we can change and discover the meaning of our own lives. So, one of the secrets of a wise and fulfilled person is his or her ability to become love to others around him or her. Thus by practicing compassion, we ourselves become compassion. That is the greatest gift we can give to ourselves.

63

The Secret of a Fulfilling Life

Leo Buscaglia puts it well, "Life lived for tomorrow will always be just a day away from being realised." One of the secrets of living a realised life is to learn to live the moment and enjoy it fully.

One of the common experiences of middle-aged or old people is that life goes too fast.

"When you are young, 60 years seems like an eternity. But after you have lived it, you realise it is but a moment" goes an old saying.

> Happiness finds us in the act of giving or acting out a bigger story.

If life goes by so quickly, then one of the ways of finding fulfilment in life is to get more out of the time we have, to find a way that each moment and each day become great gifts.

At its simplest, living the moment means to be fully there at every moment of our lives, not to judge it, but to live it.

It means we must focus neither on the past nor on the future, but experience each moment with gratitude and purpose. This means that we have the power at each moment to choose contentment and happiness. So living the moment means judging life less and enjoying it more.

Living the moment does not really mean taking each moment as it comes, it means something more significant. There was an 84-year old man actively involved in a variety of things. He would always reply to the question, "How are you?" with an enthusiastic, "I'm here!" What he really means is: "I am grateful to be alive and I recognise what a tremendous gift it is." What a contrast from many of us who would jammer: "Well, I'm here, anyway."

If time is perceived as a gift then we are grateful for it. An old scientist succinctly expressed the meaning of living the moment thus: "Every morning I wake up and say a little prayer – thank you God for another day. Being a scientist, I am in awe at existence when I think about this miracle we are living; about me as a conscious entity, here in the Milky Way with this sense and capacity. I ask God to not let me squander this day, but that as I go through my day I will be aware of what a gift it is to live. At the end of the day, before I go to sleep, I recount all the good things that happened, however small, and say thank you for this day." That is why the Roman philosopher Seneca could say: "We should count each day as a separate life."

So we need to understand that we are living our life rather than simply planning our life. If we are not careful we would find ourselves forever getting through things on our way in order to arrive at our goal or happiness. It is not that we should not plan or yearn for things we have not yet achieved or experienced. But we need to realise that happiness is always found when we are able to live in the present moment (Izzo 2008).

One of the common things we hear about terminally ill patients is that two things happen.

Suddenly, there is a sense that time is speeding by. On the other hand, they also realise that time has slowed down. Suddenly each moment and each day is treasured and lived more fully. Often for the first time in their lives nothing is seen as something to "get through."

So if we can live fully now, relish every moment gratefully. We have learnt the secret of a fulfilling life as well as death.

64

Leave Behind a Life Beyond Yourself

"An individual has not started living until he can rise above the narrow confines of his individualistic concerns to the broader concerns of all humanity," said Martin Luther King, Jr.

It is tempting to live focused entirely on one's own needs. But that does not satisfy an individual or others.

When we look at satisfied human lives, we see that people who know that they have given to life more than they took from it, have somehow stumbled onto happiness. In fact, we have a great deal of control over what we give, but almost none over what we get. Each day we have the power to give without limit. We can choose to be kind, to be generous and thus leave the world better in some way. There is something in all of us that longs to make a contribution while we are here.

While talking with older people it becomes apparent that many of us long for connection to something larger than ourselves. Giving, in fact, connects us to something larger. One physicist puts it this way: "The more I study physics, the more I believe in how much things are connected. There is a connectedness in the universe that we do not understand." Then he added, "Sooner or later you realise that you are not going to take anything with you, but you can leave something behind" (Izzo 2008).

Leaving behind, may be like a humble tree. So one biologist could say: "I can look on a map and know there are green places that will outlive me. I know that I have helped build several strong organisations that also will have a life beyond me. For some people, their legacy is their children, for me it was my work."

One of the ways of gaining insight and wisdom is to learn to lose ourselves. The loss of self is about seeing that we are connected to something much larger, something that had a life before us, and that will outlive us. So we become significant in our loss, because we are part of a larger entity. There is no better way to lose ourselves than to dedicate our life to giving, to leaving the world better than we found it.

This connects us to the future and links us to the past. This enables us to discover ourselves in the loss that we experience in our ageing and dying. Thus we can lose ourselves in the larger story and be happy.

A North American tribal story, as narrated by business author John Izzo, illustrates this. When the teenagers came back excited with a boatful of fish and handed it over to the waiting father, they were raring to go back and catch more of the fish that they had found. But the father told them, "No, we have enough already. We must leave some for others." Then the teenagers spent two days helping other tribe members mend their nets, so that they too could catch fish (Izzo 2008).

In fact, we live in a borrowed world. The fish did not belong to us. It was borrowed from generations past and held in trust for many generations yet to come. So the father taught the teenagers that giving to others is the greatest pleasure that a human being can have.

As teenagers, we believe that happiness will be found in the number of experiences we have or the possessions we gain. Later, we discover that love, service and connection to a larger purpose are the true food for the human soul. Happiness finds us in that act of giving or acting out a bigger story.

65

Happiness Lies in Feeling for Others

When asked, 68-year-old Susan gave away the secret of her own happiness: "As I have aged I find that I no longer cry for myself but I cry for the world. Part of getting older is that you realise you will not be here forever but that the story goes on beyond you" (Izzo 2008). This response shows that the happiest persons are those who cry more for the world and the unhappiest are those who still cry for themselves.

"What matters is how we treat each other and how we interact with the environment. We must think about our impact on the future," Susan added. Slowly as we age and grow in wisdom, we realise that our own problems may be serious, but there are equally serious or even more demanding problems that others have to deal with.

It is a truism to affirm that happiness cannot be pursued as such. It is a by-product of something else. As an elderly but satisfied lady put it succinctly: "If you are unhappy, get busy doing something for someone else." Thus in the process of wiping the tears of another or at least crying with others, we experience self-worth and joy.

> Our ordinary life, consisting of mundane activities, is very important for us.

As such I am not advocating crying in order to find joy. But any realistic appraisal of ours just cannot ignore the tremendous amount of suffering and toil we see around us. So all that I am asserting is that only by looking realistically at our own sorrows and those of others and giving a helping hand to those suffering more than ourselves, can we really experience genuine joy.

By being oblivious of the pain of others and seeking to remedy only our own, we are only going to experience illusory happiness or a fool's paradise.

When we do such little acts of kindness and cry for others, our own little helpful acts, in fact, create a better and nobler world. As Robert Kennedy wrote: "Few will have the greatness to bend history; but each of us can work to change a small portion of events, and in the total of all those acts will be written the history of a generation... It is from numberless diverse acts of courage and belief that human history is thus shaped. Each time a man stands up for an ideal, or acts to improve the lot of others, or strikes out against injustice, he sends forth a tiny ripple of hope, and crossing each other from a million different centres of energy and daring, those ripples build a current, which can sweep down the mightiest walls of opposition and resistance."

However insignificant we may be, we are truly called to sweep down the mightiest walls of oppression and injustice in our own little ways. That can only be done by small acts of kindness towards the poor and minor works of fighting against injustice and exploitation. Small acts of love and graciousness can contribute much towards the wellbeing of others and the world.

If I focus all the time on personal suffering and problems, I just cannot open my eyes to discover the beauty of life. But by being genuinely aware of my pain and that of others, I can truly be myself. Only when I learn to cry at the misfortunes of others, try my best to alleviate them and own them up, can I genuinely be myself.

Only by being genuinely myself which includes crying for myself and for others can I be happy and fulfilled.

66

The Power of Abandonment

In October 2009, newspapers from India reported an incredible story of a mother and a baby, born in a train toilet. The lucky child slipped through the filthy discharge chute onto the tracks. The distraught mother flung herself from the speeding train in complete darkness to rescue her baby. They were both found a few minutes later, shaken, but alive.

According to reports, 32-year-old Rinky and her husband Bhola boarded a second-class reserved compartment of the Tata-Chhapra Express from Tatanagar along with their two-year-old daughter Muskaan. Rinky was at the end of her pregnancy and Bhola, a native of Orissa's Sundergarh, wanted to get her admitted to a hospital in Sapur near Chhapra, where he works as a contractor. When the train neared Gamariah station in Jharkhand around 10.30 pm, Rinku went to the lavatory hoping to relieve her abdominal pain. Instead, she delivered the child while squatting. Before she could realise what had happened, the little figure had slipped from the birth canal and through the toilet. Rinku rushed out in panic, opened the door of the compartment and flung herself out (TNN 2009).

Bhola was unaware of the goings-on, but a few passengers and hawkers, who saw the woman jump, pulled the chain believing she was trying to commit suicide. The train stopped nearly a kilometre away. Only then did Bhola realise something was wrong. When he could not find Rinky in any of the toilets, he feared the worst and joined the passengers, who had already started a search. In the dark, they saw Rinku sitting beside the tracks, clutching her newborn.

When the train reached Purulia at 12.25 am, a medical team was ready. Rinku and the child were examined by the doctor and sent to a hospital. "This was a miracle. I have never seen anything like this in years of service," said station manager Shyama Prasad Mukherjee. Doctors at Deben Mahato Sadar Hospital were no less amazed. They could not believe that the child and his mother had survived the fall from a speeding train.

This is the second time in one-and-a-half years, that such a miracle has taken place. On February 28, 2008, a newborn girl survived a fall from a train toilet in Gujarat (TNN 2009).

In fact, Rinku and her husband Bhola represent two fundamentally different ways in which human beings respond to life. Rinku's was an instinctive abandonment out of pure love. Without counting the cost even to her own life, she dared and achieved the seemingly impossible. Hers is intrinsically a life of unconditional love, without any time to reflect. Hers is a way of life of absolute trust in someone without asking questions. Hers is a way of responding to life in a total unquestioning self-surrender and abandonment. What the Dalai Lama said is valid for her, "Approach love and cooking with abandonment." Such a person achieves miracles, even when she has to fail and give up her own life.

On the other side, Bhola is the 'normal' person, who plans, agonises and achieves things by sustained planning and hard work. This is the world of cause and effect that most of us are used to.

In fact, human life needs both. Sometimes we need to experience the power of abandonment and the emerging miracle of life. But, then, our ordinary life, consisting of mundane activities, is equally important for us.

67

Conquer Fright, Fight and Flight

In every society, there are ideal persons, the liberated ones, who are held as models for others. It may be useful for us to dwell on some basic characteristics of such an ideal person, cutting across religious and cultural boundaries.

In spite of the danger of oversimplification, we can characterise such a person as possessing genuine love, peace and joy. As suggested by Dr. Kunnumpuram, a counsellor in Patna, India, it may be heuristically helpful to appreciate these qualities when we compare them to their contraries: fear, anger and sadness.

Fear may be regarded as one of the primary human emotions. In many ways, it is useful, life-supporting and healthy. For instance, fear of the snake urges us to be very cautious when we encounter it. In fact, the basic fear against death is the cry of life to sustain itself. If this healthy fear gets out of control, we end up as paranoid. When we look within our own selves, we realise an existential emptiness (nothingness, sin, ennui, alienation, bondage), which, when not dealt with properly, aggravates fear and insecurity. So, fear is an inadequate response to our inner emptiness and becomes a terrible paralysing fright. Closely related to fear are feelings of anxiety, worry and tension.

In the hands of an authoritarian figure, with power over others, fear becomes aggression and anger. The normal dominant behaviour and aggressive anger is an overreaction to unacknowledged inner insecurity. Such fear causes fight and could be very life-threatening for oneself and others. Related feelings such as aggression, resentment, hatred and bitterness are cousins of anger, and protect us violently and unsuccessfully from our empty ego. They give us the illusion that we have power and control over others, when we do not even have it over ourselves.

Fear in the hands of someone subservient becomes sadness and depression. Since they are defenseless, they cannot fight. So they turn the fear within themselves, feeling pitiable and isolated. To get out of their fear, they have recourse to flight – from reality, from themselves and from the situation. They remain morose, gloomy and even turn schizophrenic. Unhealthy emotions of loneliness, frustration, hurt and guilt are associated with this flight from reality.

If these three basic emotions can be depicted symbolically as fright, fight and flight, their opposites suggest the vision for an integrated person.

When we confront our own basic fears and befriend them, we become capable of standing on our own and reaching out to others.

When one uses one's own strength, not to dominate or cover up one's own insecurity, the love within oneself helps one to relate to others with serenity and abandonment. Then emerges the peace that we long for: the binary opposite of anger.

Likewise, from a position of love, the sadness of the weak can truly be turned into joy or an abundance of happiness. It is the awareness that even in one's utter nothingness, one can be strong, affirmative and so accept oneself calmly and peacefully. It is an acceptance of one's nothingness that does not lead to despondency, but to tremendous power, peace and delight within oneself and with others.

In short, an ideal person is one who has encountered fear, anger and sadness and owned them up with the deepest of spiritual emptiness, leading to love, peace and joy.

68

Claude Lévi-Strauss: Exploring the Savage Mind

Claude Lévi-Strauss, the French anthropologist who transformed western understanding of what was once called "primitive man" and who towered over the French intellectual scene in the 1960s and '70s, has died at the glorious age 100.

Lévi-Strauss was an avatar of "structuralism," a school of thought in which universal "structures" were believed to underlie all human activity, giving shape to seemingly disparate languages, cultures and creations. He had a profound influence on our culture, but there has been no comparable successor to him in France.

"People realise that he is one of the great intellectual heroes of the 20th century," Philippe Descola, the chairman of the anthropology department at the Collège de France, claimed (Rothstein 2009).

His legacy is truly imposing. "Mythologiques," his four-volume work about the structure of native mythology in the Americas, attempts nothing less than an interpretation of the world of culture and custom, shaped by analysis of several hundred myths of little-known tribes and traditions. The volumes — "The Raw and the Cooked" (Lévi-Strauss 1969) "From Honey to Ashes" (Lévi-Strauss 1973), "The Origin of Table Manners" (Lévi-Strauss 1978) and "The Naked Man" (Lévi-Strauss 1981), published from 1964 to 1971 — challenge the reader with their complex interweaving of theme and detail.

In his analysis of myth and culture, Lévi-Strauss might contrast the imagery of monkeys and jaguars; consider the differences in meaning of roasted and boiled food (cannibals, he suggested, tended to boil their friends and roast their enemies); and establish connections between weird mythological tales and ornate laws of marriage and kinship.

His interpretations of North and South American myths were pivotal in changing western thinking about primitive societies. He began challenging the conventional wisdom about them shortly after beginning his anthropological research in the 1930s.

The accepted view held that primitive societies were intellectually unimaginative and temperamentally irrational, basing their approaches to life and religion on the satisfaction of urgent needs for food, clothing and shelter.

Lévi-Strauss rescued the primitive people from this limited perspective. Beginning with the Caduveo and Bororo tribes in the Mato Grosso region of Brazil, where he did his first and primary fieldwork, he found among them a dogged quest not just to satisfy material needs but also to understand origins, a sophisticated logic that governed even the most bizarre myths, and an implicit sense of order and design, even among tribes who practised ruthless warfare.

His work elevated the status of "the savage mind, " a phrase that became the English title of one of his forceful surveys, "La Pensée Sauvage" (Lévi-Strauss 1962). "The thirst for objective knowledge," he wrote, "is one of the most neglected aspects of the thought of people we call 'primitive'" (Rothstein 2009).

The world of primitive tribes was fast disappearing, he lamented. From 1900 to 1950, more than 90 tribes and 15 languages had disappeared in Brazil alone. He worried about the growth of a "mass civilisation," of a modern "monoculture." He sometimes expressed exasperated self-disgust with the West and its "own filth, thrown in the face of mankind." Lévi-Strauss liberated us from our arrogance that we are much superior to the "primitive savage" in terms of morality, aesthetics and even logic. He invited us to see the beauty and depth in our ancestors and urges us to be cautiously respectful of others.

Change and Violence

69

Stay Connected to Our Heritage

Does going back to nature solve our contemporary problems? Rousseau, Gandhi and the era of countercultural romanticism in the 1960s and 70s made people dream of the "noble savage" and a "return to nature," as a panacea for all our maladies.

For anthropologist, Lévi-Strauss, the savage was not intrinsically noble or in any way "closer to nature." He was withering, for example, when describing the Caduveo, whom he portrayed as a tribe so in rebellion against nature — and thus doomed— that it even shunned procreation, choosing to "reproduce" by abducting children from enemy tribes.

His descriptions of north and South American Indian tribes bear little relation to the sentimental and pastoral clichés that have become commonplace. Lévi-Strauss also made sharp distinctions between the primitive and the modern, focusing on the development of writing and historical awareness. It was an awareness of history, in his view, that allowed the development of science and the evolution and expansion of the west. But he worried about the fate of the contemporary culture, which was "allowing itself to forget or destroy its own heritage," as he wrote in *The New York Review of Books*. With the fading of myth's power in the modern culture, he also suggested that music had taken on myth's function. Music, he argued, had the ability to suggest, with primal narrative power, the conflicting forces and ideas that lie at the foundation of society (Rothstein 2009).

But Lévi-Strauss rejected Rousseau's idea that humankind's problems derive from society's distortions of nature. In his view, there is no alternative to such distortions. Each society must shape itself out of nature's raw material, he believed, with law and reason as the essential tools. This application of reason, he argued, created universals that could be found across all cultures and times. He is called a structuralist because of his conviction that a structural unity underlies all of humanity's mythmaking, and he showed how those universal motifs played out in societies, even in the ways a village was laid out.

Without connectedness to the past and rootedness in more contemporary myths, we are doomed.

For Lévi-Strauss, every culture's mythology was built around oppositions: hot and cold, raw and cooked, animal and human. And it is through these opposing "binary" concepts, he said, that humanity makes sense of the world.

In his "Myth and Meaning: Cracking the Code of Culture" (Lévi-Strauss 1979), Lévi-Strauss demonstrated how a structural examination of myth might proceed. He cited a report that in 17th-century Peru, when the weather became exceedingly cold, a priest would summon all those who had a harelip, or who were twins. They were accused of being responsible for the weather and were ordered to repent. Why harelips and twins? Lévi-Strauss cited a series of North American myths that associate twins with opposing natural forces: threat and promise, danger and expectation (Rothstein 2009).

Lévi-Strauss's ideas shook his field. He has clearly indicated the power of myths in shaping the views and destiny of the primitive people. He was also aware of the fading power of myths in our contemporary culture. Should we not reinvent more adequate contemporary myths that include our scientific insights and progressive religious aspirations? At the same time, we need to reconnect ourselves to our past heritage. Without connectedness to the past and rootedness in more contemporary myths, we are doomed.

70

Stir the Appetite for Thinking

As a society, do we as Indians think critically, collectively and creatively? Philosophy Talk, a weekly one-hour programme, that prides itself as a show that "questions everything except your intelligence," originates in San Francisco and its 200 episodes illustrate the appetite of the public for thinking (Reuters 2009).

The general population, who have "questions — lots of questions," are those who listen to the nationally syndicated public radio show. They call in to comment on all sorts of subjects such as violence, politics, ethics and race, wanting to share their thoughts with Ken Taylor and John Perry, both Stanford philosophy professors, and co-hosts of the talk.

> Our collective reflective, argumentative, thinking and dialogue skills need to be deepened.

Professor Taylor attributes the show's appeal to the fact that listeners find the questioning spirit of philosophy a refreshing alternative to traditional media content. Echoing that sentiment, Professor Perry adds, "Even the most thoughtful programmes on radio and television typically reach a point where they say, 'We'll have to leave that to the philosophers'. It's as if when one gets to the philosophical issues one has hit bedrock. But it's not bedrock, it's the level where you get past the mud and muck and find real gems."

Every Sunday for the past six years, the hosts have approached all manner of topics from a critical and philosophical perspective. Some topics are lofty (truth, beauty, justice), arresting (terrorism, intelligent design, suicide), and engaging (baseball, love, happiness). The hosts chat with guests and take calls from listeners, giving every broadcast a lively and conversational tone. The loyal and growing audience often carries on the discussion on internet.

Recently, scholars have noticed an increasing interest in philosophy, as evidenced by a recent New York Times article that shows an increasing enrolment in the philosophy departments of a number of colleges and universities.

Professor Perry feels that the show taps into the large, analytical segment of the population. "These are the same people who, when they hear the word 'should' they naturally ask, 'Where does that 'should' come from?' When they hear the word 'obviously', their natural reaction is 'It's not obvious to me!' Ken and I are such people, and we cater to such people" (Reuters 2009).

One of the shows will feature a top 10 list of issues or philosophical conundrums that listeners thought philosophers should tackle in the coming years. Taylor expects that the environment will rightly make one of the top lists. It is a topic that he says poses many philosophical conundrums. A recent episode about environment raised a number of compelling questions, like "What, if anything, do we owe, morally speaking, to future generations?" Further, "Do we owe it to these not yet existing people to leave them an earth as rich and as bountiful as the one we now inhabit and, if so, why?"

Why is philosophy not that well received among the Indian intelligentsia? Isn't it time India, which prides itself rightly of its profundity of thought and rigour of analytical skills, made philosophy relevant to engage with the current issues confronting us: Violence, corruption and poverty? Should not critical and collective thinking play a more crucial role in determining the policies that we make? Perhaps, despite Nobel laureate Amartya Sen's book, "The Argumentative Indian," (Sen 2005) we have become more of a "praying community" than a thinking one. Our collective reflective, argumentative, thinking and dialogue skills need to be deepened.

71

Our Collective Yearning

Ira Progoff, the world-renowned founder of "Intensive Journal Workshops," narrates an insightful experience. Returning to civilian life after World War II, and reliving the hard time in the military, Progoff lost himself in unhappy contemplation of the destructive events related to the war. In the decade from 1935 to 1945 civilisation had come precariously close to destroying itself. He began to reflect on the massive burning of books that had taken place during the Hitler era. Again and again he asked himself what would have happened to us if the ritual Nazi burning of the books had been continued until all the recorded wisdom of humanity were destroyed.

His answer was twofold. The sciences, he surmised, would be retained in the technology of the engineers. Hitler would have surely preserved the sciences, though in a stunted form, at least for the sake of making the weapons of mass destruction and for producing commodities for profit. As for the sacred scriptures of any religion, Hitler would have gladly disposed of all of them, since he had no real regard for any religion. Suppose all the scriptures of all the religions were burnt, Progoff asked himself, what would befall our civilisation?

As he lay awake, the thought struck him that humanity would draw new spiritual scriptures from the same great source out of which the older ones came. Then he became aware of how vast and self-replenishing the recourses of the human spirit are. The fires of

Hitler could burn the sacred books, but not the abiding depths out which those scriptures had emerged.

Then he questioned further: If humanity had the power to draw additional spiritual resources out of the depth of itself, why do we have to wait for a tyrant to burn our scriptures before we let ourselves create further expressions of the spirit? If it is indeed true that each human soul contains the scripture in himself, each person could contain the possibility of a new spiritual event and awareness? Perhaps, there are new spiritual insights and resources to be created by each of us as the sign of the spiritual unfoldment of contemporary society.

Contemporary world is quite different from the Vedic times. The agrarian society has given way to a technological one. The future shock has transformed our culture beyond imagination. That makes it imperative that we draw anew from our deep resources. Without in any way belittling the time-tested wisdom of ancient seers, we need to refresh ourselves from the depth of our own resources, which are in resonance with contemporary sensibilities.

For example, contemporary sensibility demands that our religion enters into a deeper dialogue with our own bodiliness and its related derivatives like sexuality, environment, health and poverty. We need a religion that responds to contemporary challenges and opportunities. So religion should not tell us to go backward and to live like the ancients. It should urge us to go forward, offering us insights and wisdom that make our lives viable.

Second, each one of us should be able to draw from our own wells, from our rich sources. Without being naively individualistic, we can individually acquire wisdom from our own self-replenishing sources that complement our collective search and respond to our current growth in technological and spiritual dimension.

Such an individual and collective drawing from our own resources will also enlarge our consciousness. Responding more to our collective yearning, we can be more authentic to ourselves.

72

Change Through Awareness

We are all in need of change — both at the individual as well as the societal levels. Our survival and success depend on the ability to initiate vital changes in our life. How do we change ourselves?

A research was conducted involving several hundred people who were trying to make simple but important changes. These people were brought together and the group was split into two. Each group was led through a process to identify the changes they wanted to make in their own lives. They were asked if they were convinced of the need to change.

The two groups were given different methods to implement the change they sought. One group set very specific goals, such as running three times a week and eating only healthy food for ten weeks. They were asked to write down these goals and review them once a week and tabulate their progress. It was thought that the process of setting specific and practical goals, reviewing them regularly and visualising the progress enabled them to change.

The second group was given a different method. They were given cards and asked to write down a few words or phrases that would remind them of the change they wanted to make. They were to carry the cards with them wherever they went for the next 12 weeks. They were also asked to look at the card and be aware of the choices they were making about ten to twenty times a day. Actually they were told never to go anywhere without the card. It was also impressed upon them that they have to be optimistic about their success and they were not to engage in any negative self-talk. It was assumed that constant reminder of the need to change, coupled with the positive outlook, made change easier.

Twelve weeks later, both groups were brought together. Both the groups had made changes, but it was found that the second group had on the whole ushered in a lot more changes. The awareness of change, constant repetition and a positive approach to change were the main factors in their success story. Through the simple act of paying attention, change happened.

It is also the natural way of a child, for instance, who learns to walk, by paying attention and experimenting. She watched, observed and experimented till she got it right. Imitation was the key to her success in walking. The positive and warm reception given by her parents also contributed to it. Learning the mother tongue is also such a natural change that occurs through awareness, imitation, experimentation and parental support. In fact, we create change by holding something before us and by experimenting with it.

Specific goal setting and sustained attempts at reaching the change normally produce the desired results, but there are many cases of "relapse" and falling back to the old habits. This may create new negativities affecting our ability to change.

On the other hand, creative and sustained level of awareness together with positive orientation of our ability to bring about such changes can create miracles. Belief in God or in a higher power can contribute to positive orientation. Such a change is possible both for individuals and society.

Today, as a society, we need to relook at our lifestyle. For example, the ecological problem confronting us is definitely the result of our dated mode of living and demands a spiritual response. Awareness of the need for a new paradigm for sustainable living, together with specific commitments, can contribute collectively to achieving the goal.

73

Awareness of Sensations

We live in a world where we fail to appreciate so many simple and ordinary events. In this context, it is truly remarkable that many people are rediscovering the virtue of awareness. Awareness of things and feelings imply that we live in the present. Awareness is an immediate experience and it cannot belong to the past or the future. Awareness is always of the instant and so of the present moment. Thus awareness of feelings, events or incidents at present enables us to be alert and awake.

We need to sharpen our sense of the presence as a present. We need to realise the remarkable gifts of life and feelings that are open to us at the moment. Instead of living in the memories of the past or plans for the future, the emphasis on the now is a welcome step in the right direction.

While meditating we also emphasise the need to be aware of our body. Unfortunately, modern men and women, in spite of the comforts at their disposal, do not pay enough attention to their bodies, emotions and desires. Thus people like Bhagawan Osho (Osho 2001) or Anthony de Mello (De Mello 1984) are right when they emphasise on awareness as key to contemporary spirituality. Many who plead for awareness of the present or the power of now, including Eckhart Tolle and Jidhu Krishnamurti (Krishnamurti 1956), trace their roots to Buddhism.

However, we need to acknowledge that the Buddhist tradition, particularly the Vipassana meditation as taught by S. N. Goenka is very clear. For him, it is not merely awareness that matters. Starting with the awareness of the breath, he stresses on the awareness of sensations all over the body. The pleasant (subtle) or unpleasant (gross) awareness on the body can be felt when we train the mind through regular and rigorous practice.

A mind thus trained can become extremely sensitive to all the nuanced vibrations that we constantly feel in the body. But he is quite clear that the ability to sense the nuanced or pleasant sensations do not in any way make one better. It is the awareness of the bodily sensations and experiencing their momentariness and becoming equanimous to them that leads us to awakening.

It is natural that when we are aware of the pleasant sensations of the body, we tend to cling to them. Similarly we tend to have an aversion for gross sensations. Constantly being aware of the nature of sensations — that they arise and disappear — makes it very clear that they are momentary. Becoming aware of momentariness of both the pleasant and unpleasant sensations we are able to get rid of the habit of clinging or detesting these sensations, making us equanimous to them. Being equanimous, we become aware of sensations without clinging to them.

Thus it is this equanimity, which liberates us from the need to cling to bodily sensations, that makes us awakened. When we are truly awakened, we live in the precious present, relishing or suffering sensations, without getting attached to them. It is precisely this ability that takes us to genuine peace, harmony and compassion.

Thus in the vipassana tradition at least, being aware of the present is important, but not enough. Being aware of the bodily sensations enable us to understand the momentariness of both pleasant and unpleasant sensations, which, in turn, will free us from our bondage, since it is the law of nature that everything passes away. In realising this truth with equanimity, we are awakened.

74

Answer Violence With a True Prayer

The atrocious bomb blasts in Jaipur, Bangalore and Ahmedabad in 2008 somehow relate religion to violence (Wikipedia_contributors 2008). Unfortunately and tragically, there are some religious fundamentalists who think they are doing a favour to their religion by instigating such violence.

When we look at the history of humanity, war and violence have been constitutive of human life. From the moment humans have evolved, a concept of self (both at the individual and social levels), competition and the consequent greed have given rise to violence. Human beings have been the most violent species when it comes to death. They are the only ones who destroy their own fellow species and kill with premeditated vengeance.

Thinkers, like Ernest Becker, trace the origin of violence to the "discrepancy or disproportion" that is unique to humans. The human imagination enables us to be creative and, in this process, there emerges a disproportion between the given and the ideal. In fact, it is this disproportion that has given rise to both religion and violence.

Becker's book, *Escape from Evil*, (Becker 1975) acknowledges that evil is mostly caused by good people bent on improving the world. In this process of fighting against evil, these good people do not hesitate to use evil. Hence, evil is nurtured in the very act of trying to eliminate it.

The recent brutal attacks on innocent civilians are to be condemned by all means. We should feel the pain of the victims and their dear ones and sympathise with them. We should definitely condemn the violence that the terrorists have caused.

> We need to be spiritually strong, morally stable or politically responsible.

There can never be a justification for such useless violence imposed on innocent people. The judicial and political apparatus of the state must do their utmost to protect the people and to punish the perpetrators of such crime.

At the same time, to claim that violence is caused by religion and that eliminating the religion will bring about a less violent society, is equally unacceptable. Realising that anything — including religion and God — can be abused is a sober religious experience. Religious people need to realise that sometimes even their religious expressions may stem from, and lead to, violence and evil.

When we look at the history of the world, it is true that religions have caused untold suffering and violence. But non-religious forces, like communism, casteism and nation-states, also have the potential for violence.

We should also realise that religion and the experience of God have a liberating potential, to make our lives on earth better and nobler. The solution to the violence perpetrated by the terrorists is to practise more of genuine religion that fosters compassion and love, by including even the "out-groups."

Can we be truly religious (or spiritual) by refusing to be part of the problem? By refusing to promote evil, even when it is masqueraded as the solution? For, genuine religions tell us that it is better for one to suffer than to cause others to suffer.

So, while experiencing the pain of the victims, let us realise the distressing fact that religion itself needs to be purified. Let us pray also for the terrorists.

75

Stopping Violence as a Religious Task

A cursory look at the Indian social and political situation opens our eyes to an alarming situation (Nussbaum 2007). Not a day passes without organised and violent attacks on people or property. Be it in Orissa, Kashmir, Karnataka or Assam, India has been going through unsettling times.

Religions, especially the organised ones, have been failing. It is true that any religion that promotes violence against one's fellow human beings covertly or overtly does not deserve to exist. Unfortunately, our religions have been failing here. Both the religious leaders and their followers have also failed miserably in safeguarding the interests of our society.

It is at this point that the state has to intervene to stem the rot. From the Indian perspective, the victims of violence are primarily our own countrymen. They are human beings first. It's only after that we can classify them as Hindus or Muslims or Christians.

So the state has a sacred responsibility to protect the life and dignity of every individual in India. The law not only has to take its course, but also has to preserve the primary quality of life of every citizen. When it is a question of protecting innocent lives no narrow political agenda or religious interests can ever come in its way. This is a sacred religious duty. It is part of the Indian dharma.

The country prides itself of being an ancient civilisation. Indians can truly be proud of the moral strength, spiritual resilience and perennial wisdom, inherent in our age-old tradition. And we can rightly look forward to being an economic superpower in the near future.

> Religion around the world can disinhibit lethal violence, by giving powerful supernatural justification.

But if thousands of innocents have to pay with their lives even in these modern times, it is simply unacceptable. When we let the situation of violence remain unabated, we are, in fact, displaying our moral bankruptcy and not our spiritual roots.

When we directly or indirectly let communal tensions flare up in various parts of the country, we are threatening the very fabric of our Indian civilisation and way of life.

The violence prevalent in the present Indian context threatens the very existence of thousands of Indians and so of India itself. Religious and political leaders in the country will be failing miserably in their duty if they let it pass for narrow political gains.

Let us treat each other with respect. Let us deal with violence firmly and gently. Let us come together and stop this insane flare-up collectively. Or else we will never be spiritually strong, morally stable or politically responsible.

The life of every Indian is precious. It would be a terrible spiritual tragedy if we let even one Indian perish for no fault of his or her. It would be a major calamity if we do not put an end to the state of violence in the present. It is a religious task. It needs political vision and determination. This is the responsibility which is imperative also for a stable economy.

76

Religion Disinhibits Violence

The relationship of religion to violence is really complex. With the possible exception of Buddhism, the world's most powerful religions give wildly contradictory messages about violence. The Christian Bible is full of exhortations to kindness, compassion, humility, mercy and justice. It also speaks about stoning, burning, slavery and slaughter. The same can be said of the Koran. The same can be said of other religious books. Believers who claim that Islam or Christianity or Judaism is a religion of peace are speaking a half truth—and a naive falsehood, as noted by Valerie Tarico in *Huffington Post* (Tarico 2009).

> Religion around the world can disinhibit lethal violence, by giving powerful supernatural justification.

The human inclination toward peacemaking or violence exists on a continuum. Happy, healthy people who are inherently inclined toward peacemaking focus on sacred texts and spiritual practices that encourage peace. Those who are bitter, angry, fearful or prone to self-righteousness are attracted to texts that sanction violence and teachers who encourage the same. People along the middle of this continuum can be drawn in either direction by charismatic religious leaders who selectively focus on one or the other.

Each person's individual violence is shaped by a host of factors: genetics, early learning, health, culture, social networks, life circumstances, etc. To blame any act of violence on religion is as silly as blaming an act of violence on guns or alcohol. But to deny that religion plays a role is as silly as denying that alcohol and guns play a role. It is to pretend that religions are ineffective, that our deepest values and beliefs about reality and morality have no impact on our behaviour.

From a psychological standpoint, religions often put a god's name on impulses that have subconscious, pre-verbal roots. They elicit peak experiences like mystic euphoria, dominance, submission, love and joy. They claim credit for the moral emotions (e.g. shame, guilt, disgust and empathy) that incline us toward fair play and altruism, and they direct these emotions toward specific persons or activities. In a similar way, religions elicit and channel protective reactions like anger and fear, the emotions most likely to underlie violence (Tarico 2009).

I argue that, like alcohol, religion disinhibits aggression rather than cause it, and that it does so only when other factors have created conditions favourable toward violence. (We can also argue that under different circumstances religion disinhibits generosity and compassion.) Millions of people consume alcohol without insulting, hitting, kicking, stabbing or shooting anyone. Most of us are peaceful drinkers and peaceful believers. Yet, statistically we know that without alcohol assaults would be less common. So too, we all know that when suicide bombings happen, religion is likely to be involved. For suicide bombings, which involve death to oneself, demands motives that are truly amazing, which probably only religion can provide.

In general, as the gospel writer said, it is far easier to see the mote in our brother's eye than the log in our own. I can see the mote in the religion of my brother than the log in my own.

Religion around the world can disinhibit lethal violence, by giving powerful supernatural justification. But to blame religion alone for violence is an easy way out, engaging in the familiar act of cowardice or scapegoating. It means, ever and always, that we end up sacrificing innocents to appease our own fear, anger and thirst for vengeance. But for us to ignore the complicated role of religion in violence is a different kind of cowardice, one that has been indulged by peace-lovers among the faithful for far too long.

The root cause of violence, I believe, lies in our own hearts, understood personally and collectively.

77

Healing Power of Prayer

Does God answer our prayers? Every believer has posed this question sometime in his life. Is God involved and interested in my personal life so deeply that he will change the course of destiny, based on my fervent request?

On the one hand it looks that God is not really interested in the individual life of one devotee. He has trillions of devotees to care for. And many a times the prayer of one devotee, if granted, may even go against the wish of the other.

Again it seems, God is concerned about the well-being of the whole universe and with its general destiny, that he just cannot get lost in details and so in the personal concerns of one private individual. So Einstein could assert: "I cannot conceive of a personal God who would directly influence the actions of individuals."

There is another argument which says that since God knows each one's needs, there is really no need to pray to God. He loves us and knows us and does the best always for us.

On the other hand, believers who have committed themselves to God, have experienced the power of prayer. Some of them have come out of shattering experiences because of the healing power of God. Throughout the history of religions, healing of individual sickness has been a hallmark of prayer.

A loving God, who does shape the destiny of the universe, cannot remain a mute spectator to the agony of the suffering of an individual.

A believer somehow knows that her prayer is heard. God answers his prayers. At the same time, he is aware that prayer of petition is only one form of prayer. There are so many other forms of prayers, that will take her closer to God and to one another.

A praying person is helped not just because he is healed spiritually. A person of faith is convinced that God listens to his personal petitions attentively. The prayers of petition cannot be explained away by saying that it is a help for "inner purification."

A believer really holds that God changes her and other's destiny because of her prayer.

Still many a time, she cannot explain, how God does not answer her prayers always.

For a person of faith, prayers of petitions are part of his larger life of prayer. He experiences that God listens to him. He also knows that God answers his prayers, not always as she wants them to be answered.

A person who prays is convinced that God answers prayers in much better ways than the devotee herself can. True God's ways are not ours. But God is on our side. He is for us. He listens to us.

Obviously prayer of petition is not the only type of prayer. There is the prayer of praise, of thanksgiving and of listening to God. There is also the prayer of contemplation and of mystical union.

But when we listen to the deep-felt cry of an innocent child, who has lost his mother in the recent terrorist blast, we definitely know that God answers his prayer.

How? We must be humble enough to admit and affirm that we do not know.

78

Beyond Individual Morality

It is often claimed that morality must be a matter of individual choice. Though applicable in a few cases, we are confronted with a larger dilemma. Can we leave it at that when collective consequences follow from our individual action?

If there is a moral imperative to protect the human race, it is not enough for us to do the right thing individually. Others must do the same as well.

But if collective consequences follow, like in the case of environmental protection or elimination of caste oppression, others must be forced to do things even if it is against their own will.

This is exactly the quality that is supposed to be so very obnoxious to moderns. The idea that morality is and must be a matter of individual choice is taken as axiomatic in modern society. It is thought to be true in the sense that it is held to describe a fact about the world.

You are entitled to your beliefs and should not be persecuted for them. But they are just beliefs and not facts. But can this sharp distinction between truth and falsity, fact and value, actually describe the world? The unexamined assumption is that we can split the world into a sphere of facts and a sphere of opinions and that the facts will speak for themselves. And, as a matter of fact, that is false. I'm not claiming here that there are no facts, or that there are only opinions, or that science is only socially constructed. I just need to point out that fact and opinion are not two distinct substances.

Often one hears: "I don't ask anyone to believe because I do, or because thousands of other scientists do. I ask you to look at the evidence." While this is an admirable ideal, it is wholly impossible to practise. You cannot believe in science if you do not believe scientists. That is why the faking of results is such a terrible threat to the whole enterprise. Nor is "evidence" a simple thing visible to the naked eye. Without quite a specialised education, the nature and force of scientific evidence is quite literally invisible. Even when the evidence is overwhelming, there will always be smart and otherwise well-educated people who ignore it if they have other more powerful reasons to do so. The instinct of most scientists is to suppose that this can be cured by teaching people science. Scientists want to be believed because the truth they are telling is so overwhelming as to make trust unnecessary. Since "the heart has reasons, which reason does not know of" in practice they will either be trusted or ignored.

So the modern conviction that to "force one's belief on someone is immoral" is itself immoral. Instances like climate change, where one's action affects the whole, makes it necessary that common moral and legal guidelines be set, even against individual's opinion. Since climate change is a danger at a global scale, individual action cannot be enough. I cannot ensure the survival of my grandchildren, or even yours, without compelling you to behave in ways that science tells me are necessary. At this juncture, not to act or not to coerce itself becomes immoral.

So in such cases where the common good is at stake, we need to go beyond individual morality and collective coercion can become imperative. Though it seems to go against the grains of modern sensibility, the common good of humanity may require such compulsion and coercion. So we need to go beyond a merely individualistic morality.

Science and Religion

79

Unlocking the Mystery of Life

"That is mystery to me!" Ordinarily we understand mystery as "something that cannot be understood." So we are called to "believe in" the mystery. Against such a "popular" understanding of mystery, philosopher Gabriel Marcel understands mystery as something so deeply significant that its meaning can only be gauged, not fully grasped. He contrasts mystery to a problem (Marcel 2001).

Unlike a problem that can be and should be solved technically or analytically, a mystery can only be encountered and experienced. Finding life on Mars is a problem, but understanding life is a mystery. Once a problem is solved, nothing of it remains. A mystery once encountered leads to deeper dimensions of it. A mystery "encroaches upon its own data, invading them, as it were, thereby transcending itself as a simple problem."

Marcel implies that mystery is a phenomenon that appears as if it can be understood through rational analysis, but the more one knows about the phenomenon, the more elusive, enigmatic and significant it becomes. Therefore, words and ideas lack the capacity to grasp fully the phenomenon of mystery. The reality of mystery can only be partially seen or understood. It can be vaguely described, but never totally revealed.

> "The most beautiful thing we can experience is the mysterious. It is the source of all true art and all science."

The mysterious cannot be fully comprehended by us. "Words allude to it; symbols express it; relationships raise our consciousness of it." But the mystery can never be wholly contained by language or meticulously categorised — like a botanist compiling a list of plants. From a spiritual perspective, we can truly agree that life is a mystery, not a problem. As a mystery, there is always more to life. Even the emptiness and pain of life has a deeper dimension (Marcel 2001).

Encountering the mysterious nature of life leads us to a gradual transformation within the perceptions, relationships, and involvements of the individual. The individual broadens her vision of the world and begins to see aspects of reality not admitted in a purely rational mindset. Once her perceptions deepen, she becomes more attentive to the needs of others and relates to people as people, not as cases or statistics.

As an individual, I have come to realise that my life — the core of my living — transcends the Self, which can be ripped apart and analysed under a microscope. The fact that I exist transcends the historical, sociological and natural forces that brought me into being and contributed to my existence. There is more to my life than my daily experiences; there is more to me than the totality of my experiences. Thus, perceiving my life as a mystery implies that I am not fully my life; I am more than my life.

As Albert Einstein would assert, "The most beautiful thing we can experience is the mysterious. It is the source of all true art and all science." He adds: "He, to whom this emotion is a stranger, who can no longer pause to wonder and stand rapt in awe, is as good as dead: his eyes are closed." Life is not a problem to be solved, but a mystery to be lived.

80

Integrating Science and Religion

Francis S. Collins is a famous American physician-geneticist noted for his landmark discoveries of disease genes and his leadership of the human genome project. He was director of the National Human Genome Research Institute. Collins has described his parents as "only nominally Christian" and by graduate school, he considered himself an atheist. However, dealing with dying patients led him to question his religious views, and he investigated various faiths. He became a believer after observing the faith of his critically ill patients and reading religious authors.

> Collins remains critical of a naive literalism found in fundamentalist groups such as Intelligent Design, which he once termed as "just ludicrous."

In his 2006 book, *The Language of God: A Scientist Presents Evidence for Belief,* (Collins 2006) Collins considers scientific discoveries an "opportunity to worship." He examines and, subsequently, rejects a narrow or fixed interpretation of religion. His own belief system is 'theistic evolution', which he prefers to term bioLogos.[12]

Collins is respectful of "earnest agnostics who have considered the evidence and still don't find an answer." But he is highly critical of agnosticism in the scientific community. "The agnosticism I see in the scientific community, which has not been arrived at by a careful examination of the evidence. I went through a phase when I was a casual agnostic, and I am, perhaps, too quick to assume that others have no more depth than I did," he says.

During a debate with biologist Richard Dawkins, Collins stated that God was the explanation of those features of the universe that science found difficult to explain and that God himself did not need an explanation since he was beyond the universe. Dawkins called this "an incredible evasion of the responsibility to explain," to which Collins responded, "I do object to the assumption that anything that might be outside of nature is ruled out of the conversation" (Time_ Magazine 2009).

Collins remains equally critical of a naive literalism found in fundamentalist groups such as Intelligent Design, which he once termed as "just ludicrous." He feels the sacred scriptures must be creatively interpreted and not literally followed. Ancient religious insights are highly valuable, provided we have the audacity to adapt them to modern scientific and social situations. He acknowledges that God's existence can't, in the end, be proved or disproved by science. And, yet, he sees "pointers to God," or natural phenomena implying the existence of the Divine.

Here are Collins' 'pointers': One, there is something instead of nothing. Two, the unreasonable effectiveness of mathematics, which makes simple and beautiful laws. Three, the Big Bang — out of nothingness, the universe came into being, which cries out for explanation, since we have not observed nature creating itself ... it causes us to postulate a creator outside of time and space, and four, the precise tuning of the physical constants in the universe. If gravity was a little weaker, things would start flying apart. You can trace a creator in these constants.

Unless believers learn to integrate modern science into their religious faith, Collins holds, they are either stuck clinging to old scientific ideas, or once they do accept contemporary science, they are in danger of having to abandon their faith out of the mistaken belief that contemporary science and creative religion are incompatible. Collins "emphasises the compatibility of religion with what science has discovered about the origins of the universe and life."

81

Science and Religion: Autonomous and Related

Francisco J. Ayala, an evolutionary geneticist and molecular biologist, who has vigorously opposed the entanglement of science and religion while also calling for mutual respect between the two, has won the 2010 Templeton Prize.

The Templeton Prize honors a living person who has made an exceptional contribution to affirming life's spiritual dimension, whether through insight, discovery, or practical work. It is the world's largest annual monetary award given to an individual, currently valued at 1 million pounds sterling. The Prize was founded by the late Sir John Templeton for significant contributions to science and spirituality and was first awarded in 1973 to Mother Teresa.

A leader in molecular evolution and genetics, Ayala has devoted more than 30 years to asserting that both science and faith are damaged when either invades the proper domain of the other. Ayala is notable because he vigorously opposes the interference of science in religion. He says that they should be kept separate because they concern different matters essential to human understanding. They can both enrich humans and contribute better to our self-understanding. They are both autonomous and related, as the life of Ayala testifies.

In his famous book, *Darwin's Gift to Science and Religion*, (Ayala 2007) he is critically appreciative of the tremendous liberative role Darwin has played for both science and religion in fostering creativity and critical mentality. While appreciating Darwin, he is also not hesitant to be critical of him, when necessary.

While he is a critic of religious fundamentalism (expressed through creationism and intelligent design theories), he holds firmly to the theory of evolution. He suggests that the theory of evolution resolves the problem of evil. So on the one hand, he does not allow his religion to influence his science or vice-versa. On the other hand, he is convinced that liberal religion and liberating religious values have much to contribute to our collective human quest.

As such science has its own autonomy, just like religion. But both science and religion have responsibility for the betterment of human beings. Knowing that science and religion have curtailed human betterment, it would be illusory to absolutise one against the other. On the other hand, when scientists and science realize their own limitations and accept critique from the larger society, it is a move in the right direction. Similarly religious leaders also have to realize the limited and necessary role that religion plays in the life of the individuals, then religion is able to relativise its own claims and so serve humanity better.

In the personal life of a scientist or a believer, it will be futile to remain in watertight compartments, with regards to our scientific openness and religious vision. As a human being the material, intellectual side of oneself has to match with the emotional and spiritual side. Though they have their own autonomies and their own laws, which are to be respected, only when one attempts to brings both these aspects to some kind of balance or harmony, can we really experience the joy of fulfilment and integration.

At the personal level, a dualistic understanding of body and soul is disastrous to personal life, just like a dualistic understanding of science and religious is devastating to our emotional and spiritual fulfilment. In our personal and collective quest for happiness and wholeness, both science and religion have different and related roles to play. They both are limited and contribute to human welfare. So we can agree totally with Fritjof Capra: "Science does not need religion, religion does not need science, but humans need both."

82

Our Bionic Future

Futurists have long speculated about merging human body and machine, especially human brain and computer. These dreams are slowly becoming a reality: Today the deaf are hearing with bionic "ears," the blind see with the aid of electrodes, an amputee is moving a prosthetic arm by thought, someone paralyzed with locked-in syndrome is "speaking" through a brain electrode connected to a computerized synthesizer.

One such bionic advance, thought-driven neural implants, could change the lives millions who are paralysed. Neural implants listen to the brain's instructions for movement, even when actual movement is no longer possible, and decode the signals for use in operating a computer or moving a robot or an artificial limb. The technology for the basic requirements - powerful microprocessors, improved filters, and longer-lasting and smaller batteries - has advanced rapidly. Years of animal research have revealed neuron activity and the brain's amazing plasticity: the ability to revise itself.

As noted by Judith Horstman in "The Scientific American Brave New Brain," (Horstman 2010) the research application has been slow. Scientists first had to determine what parts of the brain were controlling movement so they could figure out where to apply the brain wave sensors or electrodes. Several approaches have been taken, involving tapping into various places in the brain involved with the interface between muscle movement and thought.

Philip R. Kennedy and colleagues designed a device that records the neuron output. The hookup lets a stroke victim send a signal, through thought alone, to a computer that interprets it as, say, a vowel, which can then be vocalized by a speech synthesizer, a step toward forming whole words.

"Thought is gazillions of neurons firing in ensembles," affirms Kennedy. "We're trying to pick the right ones, and there's an enormous amount of trial and error" (Horstman 2010). He compares thought to a wind blowing over a vast field of wheat and his work as looking for the specific stalks of wheat that move. He has had to find a way to separate speech signals from neural noise without animal research to guide him, because no other animal speaks.

Tapping into individual neurons is next: using nanoscale fibers that could easily tap into single neurons because of their dimensions and their electrical and mechanical properties. Jun Li of Kansas State University and colleagues have crafted a brush-like structure in which nanofiber bristles serve as electrodes for stimulating or receiving neural signals. Li foresees it as a way to stimulate neurons to allay Parkinson's disease or depression or to flex astronauts' muscles during long space flights to prevent the inevitable muscle wasting that occurs in zero gravity.

A neurochip and computer backpack might allow a person to move limbs that have been stilled by spinal injury. As noted by Judith Horstman, it could open tremendous opportunities for people in the future who would like to take their minds where no man's body has gone before – into deepest space or the deepest of ocean depths, for example, through the "senses" of a thought-driven robot.

Horstman asserts that this could open tremendous opportunities for people in the future who would like to take their minds where no man's body has gone before – into highest space or the deepest of ocean, through the "senses" of a thought-driven robot.

Can such thought-driven robots enable us to perceive more the mystery of ourselves? Of thought or consciousness itself? That would be the noblest our human mind is capable of: attaining the realm of the spirit through matter. Future machine enabled bionic humans may perceive reality, including the spiritual realm, much deeper than we can currently do. That would be a blessing for us!

83

Astronomy Versus Astrology

The solar eclipse of July 22, 2009 was the longest total solar eclipse during the 21st century, not to be surpassed until June 2132 in its length and intensity. A solar eclipse occurs when the moon passes between the sun and the earth so that the sun is fully or partially covered. This can only happen during a new moon, when the sun and moon are in conjunction as seen from the earth. People, scientists, astronomers and astrologers had been eagerly waiting for this heavenly spectacle.

This was also an occasion of dispute between astronomers and astrologers. Astronomers saw it as a great scientific event, conducted experiments and drew insights from this rare phenomenon. Astrologers used it as an occasion to demonstrate the impact of heavenly bodies on human life and destiny.

I do not think that astrology can be regarded as a science. Because it does not give verifiable prediction and does not deepen human knowledge in the course of time, I refuse to see it as a science.

At the same time, I am prepared to grant some credence to some insights from astrology. People might have excitedly watched the solar eclipse early that morning, but zoo inmates went into a quiet mood, mistaking the morning darkness for dusk. In this sense, we may very well infer with astrology that all of us — including humans and non-humans, plants and planets — are far more intimately connected than we normally imagine.

Definitely, the precious prediction of the time and magnitude of the solar eclipse has been a great astronomical feat. Science and astronomy has still to perfect it and thus make human life more precise and even more perfect. At the same time, science must be humble enough to admit that there are realms in nature — including human nature — that go beyond accurate measurement and prediction. There are still areas in nature that remain mysterious and beyond the rational power of human beings — at least, for the time being. Definitely science will grow. But I do not think we can ever imagine a time where all the mysteries of nature will be explained by science.

Though there are unknowable aspects in human life, I do not think it urges us to go for the esoteric and astrology. The mistake of astrology is to make a science out of this unknowable dimension of life. The mistake of astronomy is to believe that such unknowables will one day cease to exist. Astronomers must continue to explore, with a sense of great wonder and humility. Astrologers should never exploit the unknown, and so insecure, aspects in life to create fear and insecurity.

Genuine religion and true science, I believe, must acknowledge human limitations and invite us to explore deeper the unknown, and relieve us of our anxiety, fear and insecurity. Such a humble, open-ended attitude can foster the sacredness of human life.

The inherent limit and uncontrollability of human life was best illustrated by Taregna, a village near Patna, where people gathered in large numbers to view the solar eclipse. They could watch it for three minutes, 48 seconds but were partially disappointed because of the cloudy sky, unlike in the holy city of Varanasi, India, where people had a magnificent view. We know for sure that in 123 years, there will be another great eclipse. We can predict its exact time. That is the greatness of science. But we can never be sure if it will rain then. This points to the limitation of science and the depth of reality.

84

The Truth About My Microbial Self

In a recent article in the New York Times, Olivia Judson points out that a typical human being is home to a vast array of microbes. The number of microbial cells is 10 times more than our own. On a cell-by-cell basis, we are only 10 per cent human. For the rest, we are microbial.

This has been known for a long time. Yet, it's only now, with the revolution in biotechnology, that we're able to do detailed studies of which microbes are there, which genes they have, and what they're doing. Though we are just beginning to understand this phenomenon, the results that are emerging are astonishing and profound.

It may be noted that on our skin, the diversity of bacteria is prodigious. If we were to have the hands sampled, each fingertip has a distinct set of unique residents; our palms probably also differ markedly from each other, each home to more than 150 species, but with fewer than 20 per cent of the species the same. Though scientists are still to figure out, women carry more microbial species than men (Judson 2009).

But it's the bacteria in the digestive tract, especially the gut, that intrigue us most. Many of these appear to be symbiotic to each other: they have evolved to live in guts and are most probably not found elsewhere. In providing their habitat — a constant temperature, protection from hostile environment and abundance of food — we are as essential to them as they are to us.

Gut bacteria play a crucial role in digesting food and modulating the immune system. They make small molecules that enable our enzymes to work properly. Some evidence suggests that they are essential for the building of a normal heart. Finally, it seems likely that gut bacteria will turn out to affect appetite, as well as other aspects of our behaviour, though no one has shown this yet. In fact, our gut microbes provide us with a pool of genes far larger than that found in the human genome. Indeed, the gut "microbiome," as it is known, is thought to contain at least 100 times more genes than the human genome. Moreover, whereas humans are extremely similar to one another at the level of the genome, the "microbiome" appears to differ markedly from one person to the next. The differences in "microbiome" may be due to diversity in diets, and one's own genetic background may play a role as well (Judson 2009).

Judson notes that family members tend to have more similar gut microbes than non-relatives, and preliminary evidence suggests that geography matters, too. But despite this variation at the species level, we don't yet know how much variation there is at the genetic level. It may be that different sets of gut microbes provide broadly equivalent sets of genes. Their presence may affect our health and disposition to sickness.

Such a scenario may indicate a different way of understanding human evolution. Bacteria evolve quickly: they can go through many thousands of generations for every human one. During my lifetime, my bacteria can change their genes even though I cannot change mine much. It may be that gut bacteria evolve in response to short-term changes in the environment, especially food-borne diseases and in this way further our very evolution.

It really focuses on the primary question: Who am I? How are the microbes, who live in me, part of me? How am I, who am dependent on them for essential life and genetic make-up, related to them?

85

Promote Ecology, Protect Life

In 2009, the entire nation stood behind Yugratna Srivastava as the Indian teenager addressed the UN general assembly. The only child of A K Srivastava and Roshani, Yugratna is the first girl from India, and second in the world after Severine Suzuki in 1992, to address the august gathering of over 100 world leaders, including US president Barack Obama and UN secretary general Ban Ki-moon. Speaking on behalf of nearly one billion people in her country, comprising children and youth, she addressed the general assembly session on environment conservation.

"World leaders must recognise the energy and potential which lies in children and youth. This age group is just like flowing rivers and they make their own way in the direction in which they march," said Yugratna. She did what she has been doing as a green activist – spreading awareness about sustainable development.

Yugratna is a member of Tarumitra (Friends of Trees), a non-governmental organisation devoted to stopping felling of trees and protecting forests, among other activities. It has over 16,000 schools across India as members. She was selected to address the UN session last year in Norway, where she had gone to attend the international children's conference on environment. "Over 1,200 children from all over the world had come to attend the conference," recalls Reverend Robert Athickal of Tarumitra. "So electrifying was her speech there that she was instantly picked up to represent the children of the world at the summit on climate change."

School children can be most effective in creating awareness on conservation and environment. “You just had to listen to Yugaratna to feel the kind of impact she makes through her speeches,” says Athickal from Patna, who is also an environmentalist. Yugaratna belongs to Muzaffarnagar in western Uttar Pradesh and is from St Fidelis College, Lucknow. The invite that she received from Janos Pasztor, director, United Nations secretary general’s climate change support team, recognised her endeavour in generating awareness on environment conservation. “For my generation in India, climate change means global warming, scarcity of food and drinking water and an outbreak of dreadful epidemics,” Yugaratna was quoted as saying in the UN general assembly.

Her message to Prime Minister Manmohan Singh is, “Please listen to the voices of the youth and children, and please try your best to solve all the environmental crises that are occurring in our community.”

At a time when climate change is becoming a global concern, can India show the way to protect the environment and promote life? It is a collective spiritual challenge that confronts us as a country as well as the world. The young Lucknow girl, together with R K Pachauri, chair of the intergovernmental panel on climate change (IPCC), who received the Nobel Peace prize in 2007, are symbols of India’s commitment and devotion to the environment.

We need more such citizen crusaders to save the earth, if not for ourselves, then for future generations. And India has a big role to play in this. As a British historian has observed: “It is becoming clear that a chapter which had a western beginning will have to have an Indian ending if it is not to end in self-destruction of the human race. At this supremely dangerous moment in human history, the only way of salvation is the ancient Hindu way. Here, we have the attitude and spirit that can make it possible for the human race to grow together into a single family.”

86

Guy Consolmagno: Book of Rules vs Book of Facts

Brother Guy Consolmagno, a Vatican astronomer and a practising Christian, thinks that the tension between science and religion comes from scientists who are not really comfortable with religion because they don't know it very well; the religion they know is what they learned when they were 15 years old. And many religious people are not comfortable with science because they don't know science very well. Face it, most people stopped learning science and religion when they were about 15 years old, so they have a very childish understanding of both: Religion is a big book of rules and science is a big book of facts. Fortunately, neither is true.

As children we are taught that religion is a set of ought's that must be meticulously followed so that we attain salvation. Any deviation was frowned upon. So rules, ordinances and even instructions constitute the fundamentals of religion for children. In the same vein, we were taught as children that science provides us with facts, "hard facts," uncoloured by subjective prejudices. Such facts could be relied upon, since they were accurate and always reproducible. Such facts of life, provided by science, made life comfortable and deterministic. So science provides us with what "is," while religion tells us what "ought to be."

Unfortunately, most of us remain at this level of "misinformation" till the end of our lives, and that is the cause for distress. Today study of religion and values has evolved tremendously. Theology and axiology have grown into full-fledged subjects with ancillaries. But for most believers and scientists such studies do not add anything to their own world of faith. Untouched by contemporary research and development, they cling on to their childhood religion, which most of the time may give us a false sense of security, but is surely inadequate to meet the challenges of our times. On the other hand, many true believers have become humble to accept the Divine as a profound and complex mystery, which we can only attempt to comprehend. For them, religion isn't a matter prescriptions and laws, but an intimate search to discover God and others in oneself.

On the other hand, science and technology have made stupendous progress. Though most of us are aware of it, we remain almost frightened of it. Since we have given up our scientific education at the age of 15, it is no wonder that we are still enamoured by that perfect, deterministic world that science promises. But influenced by recent scientific discoveries and philosophy of science, most of today's scientists agree that they do not have the last word. They have become humble faced with the complexity of the known world. For them, science does not give us all the facts, though science does give us the best facts accessible to us today.

To make the situation still more complex, in today's specialised world, there is hardly any practicing scientist, who is conversant with the latest in the discussion on religion and vice-versa. There are some notable exceptions. But most scientists or theologians just do not speak the same language. On the other hand, it is quite easy to see highly talented scientists with the faith of 15 year old. It is also disheartening to know that some influential religious leaders abhor science and scientific growth. Today we badly need men and women who learn science and are fascinated by its success and humbled by its dangers. We need religious people who have experienced God, are enamoured by him and realise the danger religion causes to humanity.

Concluding Words

Genuine spirituality has something directly to do with our day-to-day life and experiences. So these reflections, based on contemporary events or scientific findings, attempt to discern the spirituality present in the contemporary society.

As we come to the end of our reflections, I hope that the readers – both theists and atheists – would be kind to me in their response. My attempt has been to invite the readers to a deeper experience of every-day-events.

It is my cherished hope that these reflections will help the readers – irrespective of their religious beliefs or unbeliefs – to discern traces of beauty and profundity in everything that we experience.

Hopefully such a view of life makes us more compassionate, more humble and service-oriented. In leading such lives, we would have found meaning of our existence and opened ourselves to the Divine, that is present within us and beyond us!

Notes

1. A lakh is an Indian way of counting and it is 100,000.
2. Alain of Lille "God is an intelligible sphere, whose center is everywhere, and whose circumference is nowhere." Or Pascal: "The whole visible world is only an imperceptible atom in the ample bosom of nature. No idea approaches it. We may enlarge our conceptions beyond all imaginable space; we only produce atoms in comparison with the reality of things. It is an infinite sphere, the center of which is everywhere, the circumference nowhere. In short, it is the greatest sensible mark of the almighty power of God that imagination loses itself in that thought." See http://wadsworth.com/history_d/ special_features/ilrn_legacy/ wawc1c01c/ content/wciv1/readings/pascal1.html. Accessed on November 11,2 2012.
3. Jeffrey Stinson "Mosques increasingly not welcome in Europe" *USA Today*, 17/7/2008. Accessed on July 23, 2011. http://www.usatoday.com/news/world/2008-07-16-mosques_N.htm
4. "Will Durant." *Wikiquote,* 20 Jul 2011, 14:05 UTC. 6 Aug 2012, 04:12 <http://en.wikiquote.org/w/index.php?title=Will_Durant&oldid=1464700>.
5. Philip Goldberg, "Toward a Broader Understanding of Religion's Functions," *The Huffington Post,* April 21, 2010. Accessed on June 2, 2011. Available at http://www.huffingtonpost.com/philip-goldberg/toward-a-broader-understa_b_545314.html.
6. The full quote is: "The Religion that is afraid of science dishonors God and commits suicide. It acknowledges that it is not equal to the whole of truth, that it legislates, tyrannizes over a village of God's empires but is not the immutable universal law. Every influx of atheism, of skepticism is thus made useful as a mercury

pill assaulting and removing a diseased religion and making way for truth." Ralph Waldo Emerson, Journal entry for March 4, 1831.

7. Nilesh Nikade, "Five-year-old tortured to death for hidden treasure" Mirror Bytes: Mumbai Mirror. Accessed on 20 June, 2011. http://m.mumbaimirror.com/index.aspx?Page=article&sectname=News%20-%20City&sectid=2&contentid=20090514200905140301597842 57e8b20
8. The full quote is: "Man is the measure of all things: of things which are, that they are, and of things which are not, that they are not" Russell, B. (2009). History of Western Philosophy. Abingdon, Oxon, England ; New York, Routledge.
9. As such the shades of colour are difficult to define. See also footnote 1.
10. Here Heidegger is approvingly quoting a medieval homily.
11. "Wovon man nicht sprechen kann, darüber muss man schweigen."
12. See http://biologos.org/. The foundation defines itself as follows: BioLogos is a community of evangelical Christians committed to exploring and celebrating the compatibility of evolutionary creation and biblical faith, guided by the truth that "all things hold together in Christ." [Col 1:17]

Bibliography

Armstrong, K. (2009). *The Case for God.* New York, Knopf.

Associated_Press (2009). World's Oldest Man Dies After Life of 'Cigarettes, Whisky and Wild, Wild Women'. *New York Post.*

_______ (2010). Antony Flew Dies at 87; Atheist Philosopher Who Changed his Mind Late in Life. *Los Angeles Times.* Los Angeles.

Ayala, F. J. (2007). *Darwin's Gift to Science and Religion.* Washington, D.C., Joseph Henry Press.

BBC_Correspondent (2009 Mar 16). Physicist wins £1m Templeton gong. *BBC.*

Becker, E. (1975). *Escape from Evil.* New York, Free Press.

Blaga, L., (1980). *Gedichte = Poeme.* Bukarest, Minerva-Verlag.

Blake, W. (1976). *Selected Poems.* Norwood, Pa., Norwood Editions.

Blake, W., J. Sampson, et al. (1975). *William Blake's Auguries of innocence, together with the Rearrangement by Dr. John Sampson and a comment by Geoffrey Keynes Kt.* Burford, Cygnet Press.

Boston_University (2009). "Researchers Identify Personality Traits Of Centenarian Offsprings Which May Influence Longevity." *ScienceDaily.*

Bowcott, O. (2008 Nov 21). "16th-century Skeleton Identified as Astronomer Copernicus." *The Guardian.*

Bryanton, R. (2006). *Imagining the Tenth Dimension: A New Way of Thinking about Time, Space, and String Theory.* Regina, Sask., Talking Dog Studios.

Camus, A. (1991). *The Rebel: An Essay on Man in Revolt*. New York, Vintage Books.

Chesterton, G. K. (2007). *What's Wrong with the World*. Mineola, NY, Dover Publications.

Christakis, N. A. and J. H. Fowler (2009). *Connected: The Surprising Power of Our Social Networks and How They Shape Our Lives*. New York, Little, Brown and Co.

Clinton, H. R. (1996). *It Takes a Village: And Other Lessons Children Teach Us*. New York, Simon & Schuster.

Collins, F. S. (2006). *The Language of God: A Scientist Presents Evidence for Belief*. New York, Free Press.

Copernicus, N. (1966). *De Revolutionibus Orbium Coelestium*. Norimbergae, Bruxelles,, Apud J. Petreium Culture et Civilisation.

d'Espagnat, B. (2006). *On Physics and Philosophy*. Princeton, Princeton University Press.

__________ (2009). "Quantum Weirdness: What We Call 'Reality' Is Just a State of Mind." *The Guardian*.

De Mello, A. (1984). *The Song of the Bird*. Garden City, N.Y., Image Books.

Edamaruku, S. (2010). "The night a guru tried to kill me on TV." *The Guardian*. London.

Flew, A. (2000). "Theology & Falsification: A Golden Jubilee Celebration." *Philosophy Now*.

Flew, A. and R. A. Varghese (2007). *There Is a God: How the World's Most Notorious Atheist Changed His Mind*. New York, HarperOne.

Floyd, C. (1999). "The Limbic Fire: Neuroscience and the Soul. An Interview with V. S. Ramachandran." *Science and Spirit Magazine* 10(3): 24.

Freitas, D. (2008). *Sex and the Soul: Juggling Sexuality, Spirituality, Romance, and Religion on America's College Campuses*. Oxford ; New York, Oxford University Press.

Ghose, S. (2008 Aug 6). "Disabled, born in a nation which doesn't care IBNLive," http://ibnlive.in.com/news/disabled-born-in-a-nation-which-doesnt-care/70510-3.html, accessed on June 3, 2013.

Gibran, K. (1937). *The Prophet*. New York, A.A. Knopf.

Goldberg, Philip "Toward a Broader Understanding of Religion's Functions," *The Huffington Post*, April 21, 2010. Accessed on June 2, 2011. Available at http://www.huffingtonpost.com/philip-goldberg/toward-a-broader-understa_b_545314.html.

Grandia, K. (2009). "Taking a Stand For The Poor - Global 'Stand Up' Events This Weekend." *Huffington Post*.

Harris, S. (2005). *The End of Faith: Religion, Terror, and the Future of Reason*. New York, W.W. Norton & Co.

Heidegger, M. (1962). *Being and Time*. London, SCM Press.

Horstman, J. (2010). *The Scientific American Brave New Brain*. San Francisco, Calif., Jossey-Bass.

IANS (2009 Oct 12). "Beyond Books: CBSE to Grade Attitude and Values Too.' http://twocircles.net/2009oct12/beyond_books_cbse_grade_attitude_and_values_too.html, accessed on June 4, 2013.

Izzo, J. B. (2008). *The Five Secrets You Must Discover before You Die*. San Francisco, CA, Berrett-Koehler Publishers, Inc.

Judson, O. (2009 Jul 21). "Microbes 'R' Us." *The New York Times* http://opinionator.blogs.nytimes.com/2009/07/21/microbes-r-us/, accessed on March 3, 2013.

Keim, B. (2010 Mar 18). "Evolution of Fairness Driven by Culture, Not Genes." *Wired*. http://www.wired.com/wiredscience/2010/03/evolution-of-fairness/ accessed on March 3, 2013.

Krishnamurti, J. (1956). *Commentaries on Living*. New York,, Harper.

Kristof, N. D. (2009 Jul 2). "When Our Brains Short-Circuit." *New York Times*.

Leach, B. (2009 May 27). "Men Are the 'Weaker Sex' Says Study of Births." *The Telegraph*. London.

Lehr, D. (2009 may 16). "Bernard d'espagnat wins 2009 Templeton Prize." *Templetonprize.org*.

Lévi-Strauss, C. (1962). *La pensée sauvage*. Paris, Plon.

_________ (1969). *The Raw and the Cooked*. New York, Harper & Row.

_________ (1973). *From Honey to Ashes*. London, Cape.

_________ (1978). *The Origin of Table Manners*. New York, Harper & Row.

_________ (1979). *Myth and Meaning*. New York, Schocken Books.

_________ (1981). *The Naked Man*. New York, Harper & Row.

Levinas, E. (1979). *Totality and Infinity: An Essay on Exteriority*. The Hague; Boston Hingham, MA, M. Nijhoff Publishers.

_________ (1998). *Otherwise than Being, or, Beyond Essence*. Pittsburgh, Pa., Duquesne University Press.

Marcel, G. (2001). *The Mystery of Being*. South Bend, Ind., St. Augustine's Press.

McDonald, P. (2004). *Oxford Dictionary of Medical Quotations*. Oxford, Oxford University Press.

Mukherji, A. (2009, Oct 12). "CBSE to also Grade Values, Life Skills." *Times of India*. Retrieved from http://articles.timesofindia.indiatimes.com/2009-10-12/india/28066687_1_attitudes-and-values-r-n-podar-school-avnita-bir

Nikade, Nilesh, "Five-Year-Old Tortured to Death for Hidden Treasure" *Mirror Bytes: Mumbai Mirror.* Accessed on 20 June, 2011. http://m.mumbaimirror.com/index.aspx?Page=article&sectname=News%20-%20City&sectid=2&contentid=2009051420090514030159784257e8b20

Nussbaum, M. C. (2007). *The Clash Within: Democracy, Religious Violence, and India's Future.* Cambridge, Mass., Belknap Press of Harvard University Press.

OneWorld (2009 Oct 22). "Mammoth global anti-poverty campaign breaks world record."

Ortberg, J. (2008). *Faith and Doubt.* Grand Rapids, Mich., Zondervan.

Osho (2001). *Awareness: The Key to Living in Balance.* New York, St. Martin's Press: Distributed in Canada by H.B. Fenn and Company.

Padinjarekara, F. J. (2009). *A Dewdrop in the Ocean: Wisdom Stories for Turbulent Time.* Mumbai, Awareness Arc Publishing.

Pandikattu, K. (1996). *Idols Must Die so that Symbols Might Live: Towards an Ontology of Ricœurian Symbols.* Faculty of Theology. Innsbruck, University of Innsbruck. PhD Thesis.

_________ (1999). "Human Freedom: The Finite Quest for the Infinite." *Jnanadeepa: Pune Journal of Religious Studies* **2**(2): 127-149.

_________ (2000). *Idols to Die, Symbols to Live: Dynamic Interaction between Language, Reality, and the Divine.* New Delhi, Intercultural Publications.

_________ (2009). "Ever Approachable, Never Attainable: Scientific and Philosophical Reflections on the Human Person." *Omega: Indian Journal of Science and Religion* 8(1): 62-79.

Pausch, R. and J. Zaslow (2008). *The Last Lecture.* New York, Hyperion.

PennLive (2008 Oct 5). 'Religulous' Challenges Preconceived Notions about Science and Religion. *PennLive.*

Peregin, C. (2009 June 22). "University Students Opting for Broader Sense of Spirituality." *Times of Malta.*

Peter, T. (2008) *Speaking to, Speaking of, Speaking about the Ultimate in our Theological Quest for Human and Cosmic Fullness.* Faculty of Theology. Innsbruck, University of Innsbruck. PhD Thesis.

Plato and D. Gallop (2009). *Phaedo.* Oxford ; New York, Oxford University Press.

Rawls, J. (2005). *A Theory of Justice.* Cambridge, Mass., Belknap Press.

Reuters (2009). "200 Episodes of 'Philosophy Talk' Radio Show Illustrate Appetite for Thinking." *Reuters.*

Ricœur, P. (1967). *The Symbolism of Evil.* New York,, Harper & Row.

__________ (1996). "Arts, Language and Hermeneutic Aesthetics: Interview with Paul Ricoeur." *PHILO RECHERCHE - FAC.* B. Jean-Marie and M. Uhl.

Rothstein, E. (2009 Nov 4). "Claude Lévi-Strauss, 100, Dies; Altered Western Views of the 'Primitive'." *The New York Times.*

Rodriguez, Rene. (2008). "Review of Religulous." The Charlotte Observer. Retrieved July 23, 2013, from http://www.zvents.com/reviews/show/31558-maher-comes-across-as-ridiculous-in-religulous

Russell, B. (2009). *History of Western Philosophy.* Abingdon, Oxon, England ; New York, Routledge.

Schneiders, S. (1986). "Theology and Spirituality: Strangers, Rivals, or Partners." *Horizons* 13(2): 253-274.

Schroeder, G. L. (2001). *The Hidden Face of GOD: How Science Reveals the Ultimate Truth.* New York, Free Press.

Sen, A. (1999). "Democracy as a Universal Value " *Journal of Democracy* 10(3): 3-13.

__________ (2005). *The Argumentative Indian: Writings on Indian History, Culture, and Identity*. New York, Farrar, Straus and Giroux.

Sen, A. (2009). *The idea of Justice*. Cambridge, Mass., Belknap Press of Harvard University Press.

Seyfried, E. (2010). *Unhaling: On God, Grace and a Perfectly Imperfect Life*, Venia Press.

Singh, J. (2009). *Jinnah: India, Partition, Independence*. New Delhi, Rupa & Co.

Jeffrey Stinson "Mosques increasingly not welcome in Europe" *USA Today*, 17/7/2008. Accessed on July 23, 2011. http://www.usatoday.com/news/world/2008-07-16-mosques_N.htm

Steiner, G. (1991). *Martin Heidegger*. Chicago, Ill., University of Chicago Press.

Tarico, V. (2009 Dec 1). "Like Alcohol, Religion Disinhibits Violence, Doesn't Cause It." *Huffington Post*.

Templeton_Report_Correspondent (2009 Apr 15). "Bernard d'Espagnat's "Ultimate Reality."" *Templeton Report*.

TempleUniversity (2008 Oct 26). "Spirituality Protects Against Depression Better Than Church Attendance." *ScienceDaily*.

Time_Magazine (2009 July 9). "God vs. Science - A Debate between Richard Dawkins and Francis Collins."

TNN (2009 Oct 8). "Newborn falls off train, survives." *Times of India*.

Tolle, E. (2004). *The Power of NOW: A Guide to Spiritual Enlightenment*. Vancouver, B.C., Canada Novato, Calif., Namaste Pub. ; New World Library.

__________ (2005). *A New Earth: Awakening to Your Life's Purpose.* New York, N.Y., Dutton/Penguin Group.

University_of_California_San_Diego (2010). "Acts of Kindness Spread Surprisingly Easily: Just a Few People Can Make a Difference." *Science Daily.*

Walls, L. D. (2003). *Emerson's Life in Science: The Culture of Truth.* Ithaca, N.Y., Cornell University Press.

Waters, B. (2006). *From Human to Posthuman: Christian Theology and Theology in a Postmodern World* Hampshire, Ashgate.

Weinberg, S. (1993). *The First Three Minutes: A Modern View of the Origin of the Universe.* New York, Basic Books.

Whitehead, A. N. (1925). *Science and the Modern World: Lowell Lectures, 1925.* New York,, The Macmillan company.

Whitehead, A. N., D. R. Griffin, et al. (1978). *Process and Reality: An Essay in Cosmology.* New York, Free Press.

Wikipedia_contributors (2008). "2008 Bangalore Serial Blasts." *Wikipedia, The Free Encyclopedia.*

__________ (2012). "Big Five Personality Traits." *Wikipedia, The Free Encyclopedia.*

"Will Durant." *Wikiquote,* . 20 Jul 2011, 14:05 UTC. 6 Aug 2012, 04:12 <http://en.wikiquote.org/w/index.php?title=Will_Durant&oldid=1464700>.

Wittgenstein, L. and C. K. Ogden (1990). *Tractatus logico-philosophicus.* London ; New York, Routledge.

Ziglar, Z. (2002). *Raising Positive Kids in a Negative World.* Thomas Nelson Inc.

Index